Redefining the Subject

GENUS:
Gender in Modern Culture

2

Russell West (Berlin)
Jennifer Yee (Newcastle-upon-Tyne)
Frank Lay (Cologne)
Sabine Schülting (Berlin)

Redefining the Subject
Sites of Play in
Canadian Women's Writing

Charlotte Sturgess

Amsterdam - New York, NY 2003

The paper on which this book is printed meets the requirements of "ISO
9706:1994, Information and documentation - Paper for documents -
Requirements for permanence".

ISBN: 90-420-1175-0
©Editions Rodopi B.V., Amsterdam - New York, NY 2003
Printed in the Netherlands

For Dominique

Acknowledgements

I wish to thank the Canadian Government for its generous support in according me a grant in order to carry out research in Canada.

I also wish to thank the English department of Marc Bloch University, Strasbourg, for their understanding and practical help, in particular when it came to arranging my teaching schedules.

Table of Contents

INTRODUCTION 11

COLLECTIVE VOICE: HISTORY AS SUBJECT 19

Hiromi Goto, *Chorus of Mushrooms*:
Tracks in a Textual Landscape 19

Anne Michaels, *Fugitive Pieces*: Geo-Logical Retrievals 34

ROUGH CROSSINGS: DISPLACEMENTS,
DESTINATIONS AND APPROPRIATIONS 51

Dionne Brand, *Sans Souci* and *In Another Place,
Not Here*: a Poetics of Migrancy. 51

Suzette Mayr, *The Widows*: Kanada/Canada, Bridging the Gap 65

THE FEMALE SUBJECT AS "OTHER":
SYMBOLIC LOCATIONS AND DISLOCATIONS 77

Evelyn Lau, *Other Women* and *Runaway:
Diary of a Street Kid*: Consumer Culture, Exotic "Other" 77

Nicole Brossard, *Mauve Desert*: Crossings and Sitings 89

GEO-POLITICAL MAPPINGS: DISTANCE AND DIFFERENCE 99

Aritha van Herk, *Places Far From Ellesmere*:
Place, Perception, Self 99

Kristjana Gunnars, *The Prowler*: Territorial Rights, Textual Ways 109

GENRE AND GENDER-BENDING 121

Margaret Atwood, *Wilderness Tips* and *Good Bones*:
Myths Revisited, Value Added 121

Susan Swan, *The Wives of Bath*: the Female Body in Question 133

CONCLUSION 143

WORKS CITED 147

INDEX 155

Introduction

The particular history of Canada could be seen as one of ambivalence and hesitation. Founded through strong and enduring ties to Europe and in recent decades to the United States, Canada's bilingual political reality and a cultural imaginary of two solitudes gave way, with the arrival of succeeding waves of immigrants, to representation as a "mosaic" and, more recently, to an officially ratified politics of multiculturalism. The search for an "authentic" Canadian literary identity likewise evolved; Robert Kroetsch and Margaret Atwood among others expressed a suspicion towards the metanarratives of a neo-colonial history. Kroetsch set about to "unwrite" the social, political and cultural "written" of a national space founded in "a concealed other experience, sometimes British, sometimes American" (1983, 17). Atwood coined the enigmatic phrase "home ground, foreign territory" (1979, 11) to render the aporia at the centre of the Canadian ontological dilemma. As Atwood investigated in *Surfacing* the Canadian filiations and affiliations to Empire and North American capitalism, which hampered a viable Canadian self-represention, she equally pointed the finger at those phallogocentric cultural narratives which deny women full representative status.

Since the 1970's, theoretical perspectives on both female identity and national identity have evolved and diversified. French feminist theory, with its philosophical underpinnings, grounded in the female body as the site of difference, has cohabited with, and often confronted, theories of agency grounded in the material conditions of a "lived" reality. Likewise, Canadian cultural criticism and postcolonial theory at large has indicted the neo-imperialisms lurking behind the apparent political generosity regarding claims for equal rights. Critics such as Arnold Harrison Itwaru, Roy Miki and Smaro Kamboureli have challenged what they see as a Canadian version of the enlightenment paradigm, one which they claim has engendered a politics of multiculturalism founded through an ideology of progress based on a liberal economy, which tends towards a recuperation of the "ethnic other" for its own ends. The all-inclusive tolerance traditionally attributed to Canadian social and political policies, exemplified by the Multiculturalism Act of 1988, which officially recognized Canada's ethnic diversity, has been criticized as seeking to contain (see Kamboureli 2000, chapter 2), rather than promote difference. The dominant Anglo-Saxon model of Canadian culture is, according to many of the recent voices in literary and criticism, still an implicit norm. Equally, the idea of a Canadian literary imaginary presenting "identity ... [as] something which one steps into, like a pair of shoes" (Itwaru 1990, 26) has been criticized as the bias of a dominant Anglo-Saxon voice which cannot account for, and does not accommodate, writers from different ethnic and racial backgrounds and different social configurations. The increasing challenge to the Canadian "ideal" of a benevolent, open society, has thus, in recent decades, split open the dualistic English/Canadian model of representation.

Such insistent questioning of the premises on which Canadian "identity" has politically, culturally and imaginatively been elaborated has inevitably led, in the wake of post-structuralist, postcolonial and feminist theory, to an increasing challenge to the concept of "identity" itself. The idea of a unified Canadian cultural space, whether that of a "mosaic" or of a "multicultural" ideal, has given way to the recognition of "identity" as a construct, as a discursive field of power relations, divergent group interests and personal equations, in which the nation state represents "the arrival at a point of departure in the continual search for social meaning" (19). The country "Canada", perceived in this light, is the mobile sign of a continual and uncloseable "search for Canada" (19), in its social, political and cultural dimensions.

Yet if, in this new millenium, boundaries of monolithic versions of Canadian identity have been severely tested, the need for personal and political agency on other terms has become increasingly crucial. Since, as master narratives of both imperialism and its brother-in-arms phallogocentrism are deconstructed, the terms on which change can be effected and become effective are increasingly problematical. For if there is no longer a stable, "authentic" position to be held in the realm of politics and culture, the emergence of different interests and valid claims for recognition has made of cultural positioning itself the major field of inquiry. If, therefore, "identity" as a belief in an "out there" of an either present or recoverable, ideologically unified Canadian nation state has collapsed, the concept of identity has not been jettisoned but has instead fractured and proliferated. "Identity" is no longer to be seen, or theorized, as an unmediated, fixed link between nation and individual, but as a negotiation of subject positions within a network of material forces affected and inflected by class, gender and race.

This has entailed an increasingly intense investigation into the meaning and deployment of subjectivity in the fields of social and political, but also literary and artistic representation. Subjectivity is here to be understood according to the broad definition given by Rosi Braidotti as "neither a biological nor a sociological category but a point of overlapping between the physical, the symbolic, and the sociological" (1994, 4). Stressing the roots of subjectivity in bodily desires, and the structuring of the subject through his/her emergence in language, Braidotti states that "[t]he acquisition of subjectivity is ... a process of material (institutional) and discursive (symbolic) practices, the aim of which is both positive – because they allow for forms of empowerment, and regulative – because the forms of empowerment are the site of limitations and disciplining" (99). In that such a definition takes in both material (historical and "lived") and symbolic (the imaginary identifications which our entry into language both forecloses and maintains) forces, it situates the subject at the centre of a network of multiple discourses. "Subjectivity", or "identity", (since my purpose is not to analyse the various ways theorists use the two terms, but to invite an acceptation of their discursive underpinnings which my own readings rely on), is thus the way the self both shapes and is shaped through language, within the multiple discourses in which one participates.

Nevertheless, the object of this critical study is not only the links between Canadian fictional representations and national ones, it also seeks to frame both within the claims to representation – those symbolic and material forms of empowerment cited earlier which are equally the site of limitations – of women's writing.

For, just as Canadian national self-representations have come under pressure, so women's specific interests and claims in society have diversified. The concept "women's rights" has given way to a consciousness that there is no monolithic discourse of equality, that race, class, education and a network of other factors can enter into the equation, inflecting one's positioning in society. In Canada, in particular, given the recent emergence of women's literary and theoretical voices from ethnically diverse sectors of the population, the representation of a unified feminine "selfhood" or claim for recognition, has increasingly been challenged. Given the breakdown of a unified political and social agenda, the notion of a single version of "female identity", for which recognition is to be sought, has itself collapsed.

Traditionally marginalized, performing on several "stages" of social and symbolic representation simultaneously, women have developed an exacerbated awareness of how phallogocentric culture functions. It is therefore not surprising that their problematical access to rights and their implication in both discourses of exclusion and inclusion have given rise to an increasing theorisation and imaginative investigation of the place of the female subject in the language(s) which mediate(s) her positioning(s) in society. Canadian women's writing can thus be seen to be strategically positioned in a conflicted cultural imaginary which is frequently regarded as gendered, since, as Barbara Gabriel remarks: "[i]t has become a cliché to note the Canadian ambivalence about nation-making in contrast to the United State's wholehearted enthusiasm for its own expansion" (1994, 39). The place of "Woman" as the negative "Other"of both social and political as well as symbolic (thus textual) representations, is in no way synonymous with Canada's symbolic and ideological "Othering", since there is no one, single structuring of "Woman" in society and no one version of "Canada". It nonetheless allows for interesting overlappings, as I hope the following analyses of texts from very diverse personal and political locations will demonstrate. Furthermore, although there is no single version of women's writing in a postcolonial context, such writing does clearly reveal certain common features: a consciousness of boundaries, of the binary oppositions structuring gender and culture, of discontinuities, of historical and cultural silencing and the effort to come to voice, of the stakes in play through the collusion of fictional representation with an authoritative *telos*.

If we posit that all writing, whatever its ostensible object, is inevitably an expression of subjectivity, and if all subjectivity is a "fiction" – structured in language – then the focus of the study which follows is the interaction between the self in fiction and those fictions of the self which emerge from, and feed into, a specifically Canadian imaginary. My object is to investigate the ways in which women's writing constructs Canada as an unstable reference, as a site of social, historical and symbolic overlappings, just as female subjectivity is constructed through similar discursive modalities. The textual, aesthetic negotiations at the core of these transactions may differ; they all however demonstrate in some way that "Canadian discourse", like women's writing, is the "discourse of the Other" a "rise of the repressed, dislocating and undermining the logic of the literary systems of the Anglo-American world" (Godard 1987, 44). The "hybridization and dissemination" (44) at the centre of Canadian writing, a literary production inscribing marginality in its very textual modalities thus stage "identity" as "difference", as a continual play of allegiances and perspectives. The chapters which follow are therefore not only concerned with how women's writing interrogates and seeks to redefine the place of women in culture and history, they equally open onto redefinitions of Canadian narratives of the nation in all its complexity. They explore the diverse ways in which Canadian women's literature is always in excess of, and disruptive of, any monolithic interpretation of nationhood and of subjectivity, as constituting not only a different kind of writing but a literature of "difference" itself. Canadian women's writing is thus one of thresholds in all senses of the word: cultural, ideological, personal and, inevitably, textual. This volume attempts to focus on some of those thresholds in their aesthetic and cultural dimensions.

Most of the works examined here are fiction, with one exception: the diary *Runaway*. Most of the writers are English-speaking, with, again, one exception, Nicole Brossard: I took the lead from Bhakhtin's *heteroglossia,* not only allowing myself the freedom of cutting across Canadian linguistic borders, but, in the case of the non-fiction text, the diary, across generic ones. Furthermore, although many of the texts share in some way the loaded appelation "ethnic", speaking from a cultural positioning which has been theorized variously as "hybrid" "hyphenated" and "cross-cultural", the very variety of their imaginary responses to such appelations precisely sheds light on the way culture is not a given form of representation but an unstable one, dependent on location (in the language, society and ideology of the country one lives and works in). In this respect, whereas the Caribbean-Canadian Dionne Brand actively seeks in her work to graft historical prejudice and injustice onto a poetic aesthetics, the Chinese-Canadian writer Evelyn Lau seemingly renounces any form of community responsibility, for which she has been severely criticized. Other writings in the collection, those of Susan Swan or Margaret Atwood for example, come from radically opposed cultural horizons. Their fiction takes as a point of departure their personal location as Anglo-Canadian feminists; it is characterized by irony, often deployed as an overt challenging of phallocentric discourses. However their forms of textual alterity do not, like Brand's or Hiromi Goto's, stem from a consciousness of racial difference, or from the inherently split perception of those ethnically marginalized. They do however, seek to confront a Canadian liberal discourse with its own limits and focus on those power relations that are a function of gender relations, that is, the way the female body is the site where the binaries Nature/Culture, Self/Other are played out.

The volume is divided into six chapters, each one discussing works of two writers. This was motivated by a wish to highlight the diverse imaginative and aesthetic engagements of the texts in question, but also to foreground shared concerns and responses. In the first section, Anne Michaels and Hiromi Goto are paired together, despite their disparate backgrounds and the divergent thematic foci of the respective texts, as both problematize the role of language in dealing with the loss and recovery of memory and community voice. Both also investigate the scars left by the Second World War on later generations.

"Rough Crossings", the following chapter, is an oblique reference to the Caribbean "middle passage" – the sea route transporting slaves to the West which has been used a powerful metaphor of uprooting and exile. "Crossing" however, also signifies "arrival", and this informs us of the accommodation made by the displaced communities in the interest of a Canadian cultural hybridity Dionne Brand's Caribbean-Canadian status is reflected in the resistance poetics of the stories and novel under scrutiny here; cultural hybridity is an often traumatic limit drawn within resistance to White hegemonies. Whereas *The Widows* brings out the links and discontinuities that necessarily cohabit; the negotiations to be made between codes of Europe and those of a New World (which proves, in its prejudices, to be not so new after all), between social propriety and the disruptive impropriety characterizing the migrant's reality.

The next section centres on female subjecthood as symbolic erasure and as symbolic, textual relocation, examining how Lau's diary constitutes an "unruly" autobiographical account. On the other hand, van Herk's autobiographical narrator symbolically relocates within what she calls *geografictione* – a close encounter between "place" and female subjecthood within language itself.

In the following part, the "translation" tactics of Nicole Brossard, the only Quebecois writer in the volume, and those of the Icelandic-Canadian Kristjana Gunnars, produce fictions of multiple limits and boundaries. I intend to demonstrate how the aesthetics and politics of their ontological and epistemological "crossings" transform the familiar into a space of feminine "difference", destabilizing both linguistic conventions and Canadian imperialisms.

Lastly, Susan Swan and Margaret Atwood work the seams of genre and challenge discursive constructions of gender. The writings under scrutiny interrogate the power plays and binary oppositions structuring gender and the marginalized status of women in such oppositions. I concentrate here on how their writings manipulate iconic representations and popular cultural forms, how they deploy ambivent encodings in order to undermine the hierarchies sustaining notions of value as well as Canadian national mythologies.

The general aim of the following study is thus to show that if "the personal is the political", then the "personal" of Canadian women's writing, in its aesthetic dimension, opens up the "political" to reappraisal, shifts its discursive moorings and challenges its ideological premises. At the same time, modes of feminine representation within culture and language are reworked and recontextualized. The revisionary potential which such writing deploys, seeking to inscribe new meanings in the interstices of representation, or tranforming existing literary models and imaginary forms, points to the radical drive of such enterprises. The result is often a state of fertile "in-betweenness", as thresholds of being and access to expression are continually negotiated and reassessed.

Collective Voice: History as Subject

Hiromi Goto, *Chorus of Mushrooms*: Tracks in a Textual Landscape

> There is a silence that cannot speak.
> There is a silence that will not speak (Kogawa 1981, preface).

The Japanese-Canadian Joy Kogawa, author of *Obasan*, the novel cited above, recounts the fate of the Japanese community in Western Canada during the Second World War, when Pearl Harbour led to the tracking, uprooting and internment of ninety percent of the Japanese-Canadian population, judged "enemy aliens". Hiromi Goto, another Japanese-Canadian, looks at the trauma of war and uprooting from a different perspective in *Chorus of Mushrooms*. If the theme of war in Goto's narrative concerns rather the uprooting and displacement of the community in Japan itself, seen through the personal history of the grandmother in the narrative, both these Japanese-Canadian novels emphasize the split between public and personal reality, between overarching political decisions and community sufferings. As Keibo Oiwa has stated: "most of the writings on Japanese-Canadian history have ... been 'a history in passive voice' ... It is as if the history of the persecuted could be reduced to what their persecutors did" (1991, 15).

It is with this erasure that *Chorus of Mushrooms* takes issue, and does so through strategies which foreground the links between language and identity; between cultural silencing and personal silence within three generations of a Japanese-Canadian family. The novel is concerned both with possible alternative narratives of Canadian identity and also with the female subject's place in such alternative versions. *Chorus of Mushrooms* equally addresses a Canadian, cultural mythology which, as Frank Davey has remarked, speaking on contemporary English Canadian fiction, paradoxically combines the "questioning of Eurocentric historiography's appropriateness to non-European, non-white or non-male experiences", while remaining "a

fiction of white, male, Canadian-born writers" (1997, 24). As Davey
puts his finger on the irony of national, literary representations of
selfhood of the Canadian West, he voices the challenge which *Chorus
of Mushrooms* rises to, that of exploring and remodelling those Canadian mythologies which, if differing from the American "great frontier" narrative of the "search for the missing myth [of origins]"
(Davidson 1994, 17), remain nonetheless attached to the literary script
of an "authentic" (if failed), male subject of Canadian representations.

If the "Canadian Western's preference for Other stories" (15) has
resulted in a concerted playing with the conventions and ideological
presuppositions of the hero-centred Western narrative of expansion
and exploration, while nonetheless maintaining the implicitly male
subject of such narratives in place, Hiromi Goto's female-centred
chorus reinvents this Canadian West as "Other". Goto's novel is neither a lamenting, nor a search for an implicitly Oedipal, stable source
of identity. It proposes the exploration of a personal and textual territory which is both hybrid and multiple, thus subverting the teleology
implied in both origin-centred and origin-lacking narratives.

To this end, the "chorus" of Goto's title aptly signals the undermining of a unique narrative consciousness. It also points to this collective voice – strangely assigned to "mushrooms" – as taking on
paradoxical dimensions. In revising a Canadian cultural mythology
and by inscribing a hybrid community space at the centre of its textual
strategies, the novel seeks to undermine notions of "culture" as a transcendent metanarrative inspiring and reflecting an essentially masculinist world-view. It thus displaces globalizing versions of history, and
re-places the subject at the centre of his/her story, emphasizing precisely the *situatedness* of all recitations of the self, the way language
and culture interact within the local, personal domain of the subject's
experience.

The Little House on the Prairie: Myths of Origin Revisited

The classic image of man against a hostile environment is, according to Margaret Atwood a founding projection of the Canadian literary
imagination (1972, 32). Atwood's version of the founding traits of
Canadian literature has not gone uncontested, mainly on the grounds
that such an interpretation elides other versions of Canadian culture to
serve specifically Anglo-Canadian perceptions. However, if this is the
case it merely amplifies the issue of rewriting here, demonstrating the
"wilderness" myth as a fabrication of a Eurocentric perception of
Canada. Contrary to the American ethos of frontier expansion, the

"garrison mentality" is a marker of cultural anxiety, just as it participates in the myth-making of Canadian collective identity. Within this
mythology of the hostile outdoors, the West has been conceptualized
as the "degree zero of national space" as a horizontality which "is the
epitome of an imperialist dimension" (Gabilliet 1996, 202-3, translation mine), in that it opens itself up to imaginary and colonizing appropriations. Woven in and around Canadian prairie geography is
therefore a literary history and a set of representations which *Chorus
of Mushrooms* both echoes and subverts. In his canonic *As For Me
and My House*, the forefather of prairie literature, Sinclair Ross, ex-
ploits the point of view of his female character Mrs Bentley in order to
relate "the precariousness of the town and herself" in an artistic vision
where "[m]an and environment are totally integrated" (Ricou 1973,
82-7).

Decades later, *Chorus of Mushrooms* presents a very different
imaginary landscape. The novel is a challenge to such "integrated"
visions, both to the transcendent merging of man and prairie in Ross's
novel, and the doubling of that transcendent vision in Laurence Ricou's critique cited above, which maintains that vertical man "erect"
in an eternal embrace with "his" landscape. Ross's female character,
whose diary – and therefore whose vision – the novel ostensibly presents, remains imprisoned in the binary opposition female/house,
male/horse of this vision: stasis versus motion, domestic enclosure
versus freedom, passive nature versus the civilizing, moral Word. As
Western Canada's "paradigmatic text" because it is a missing text
(Kroetsch 1983, 47), its blocked horizon in a town called Horizon, its
inmates in search of a narrative of origins, *As For Me and My House*
presents a founding example of a masculinist, Eurocentric prairie
imagination.

Chorus of Mushrooms can in contrast be seen as a radical, and
feminine departure from such a vision, – a literary departure which
Aritha van Herk's *No Fixed Address*, in its imaginary "remapping" of
the West as feminine space, instigated in the eighties. Hiromi Goto,
relating the story of three generations of Japanese women, her narrative spanning both the displacements and migration of the Second
World War and the personal displacement of arrival and settlement in
Canada, turns away from the straight and narrow – moral and masculine – path leading to the grail of unique origins. The cacophony of
female voices occupying narrative space, the conflicts and merging of
perspectives and the playing with iconic representations of the West,
displace the nostalgic search for the Father of the Western, Eurocen-

tric narrative; a West which van Herk has ironically named the "king-dom of the male virgin" (1992, 90).

Yet when the grandmother in Goto's novel moans a litany to the Alberta wind, the narrative reverberates strangely with the ghost of Ricou/Ross's Mrs Bentley, pitting herself against the environment when she intones: "It's been nearly dark today with dust. Everything's gritty, making you shiver and setting your teeth on edge" (Ross 1957, 62). The grandmother Naoe's "unrelenting, dust-driven dry wind" (Goto 1994, 3) here serves as an uncanny retrieval of that prior liter-ary, feminine presence. There is a dialogic aspect to such discursive traces when the grandmother's voice itself becomes at times a con-flicted, cross-cultural space of meaning, for example when Shake-speare is brought to bear to combat the wind. Hamlet's "To be or not to be" then becomes "Someone, something must stand against this wind and I will. I am" (5). Such layering of references feeds into Rob-ert Kroetsch's definition of prairie literature as literary, epistemologi-cal "archeology" (1983, 76). Citing the essential heterogeneity of a Western Canadian literary tradition, and its roots in orality, Kroetsch states: "Archeology allows for discontinuity. It allows for layering. It allows for imaginative speculation" (76). (Kroetsch's use of the con-cept of "archeology", as he states, owes much to Foucault. For an analysis of prairie literature and its attendant cultural anxieties see Kroetsch's "The Fear of Women in Prairie Fiction: An Erotics of Space" (1983, 47-56).

Feminine representation in Goto's novel is both informed by this oral, layered, aspect of the Western imaginary, and revises it, since the representation of the "house on the prairie" is brought to accommo-date the multiple conjugations of a Japanese-Canadian identity.

Yet if Ross's "House of Bentley" (Harrison 1977, 135) takes up and explores in its own fashion the metaphor of the "garrison", the pio-neer/settler response to an alien Canadian landscape, the "house of Goto" also problematizes points and modes of settlement. However, this does not entail the reinscription of codes belonging to a loved and lost Europe, but, instead, the ambivalent, multiple focus establishing contact points between Eastern and Western world views. The grand-mother remains literally immobilized in the hallway during the first part of the novel, at the cultural crossroads between prairie wind and internal dispute with her daughter, thus metaphorically standing on the border between East and West. As such she articulates a similar "gar-rison" anxiety of environment, refusing both the reality of life in Can-ada and the language which goes with it; when she comments on the incessant wind and registers the conflicts within the household, she functions as the embodied limit drawn between disparate worlds; as she nostalgically mourns the loss of an Edenic Japan where the wind was a soft spring breeze, she transforms the Anglo-Canadian pioneer narrative of settlement to accommodate other versions.

Yet it is Naoe who, in the latter part of the narrative, breaks out of the "garrison" and effects a radical rewriting of that prairie mythos of "man and horse", "woman and house". When she refuses to speak English while her daughter takes refuge in refusing all that is Japanese and the grand-daughter Murasaki navigates a difficult path between the two, the household itself also reinvents "the garrison" as a complex of intersecting linguistic enclosures attached to the various women's self-representations. The cultural and personal configuration of this prairie space is rendered in the metaphor of the house itself: "built in High River and ... the whole creaking mess hauled in a flatbed truck ... The belly of the house getting so much stress that they couldn't squeeze it back together again" (Goto 1994, 164).

Thus, unstable and displaced, the house on the plains is a sign of/for the negotiation of boundaries and their difficult resolution, accommodating a specifically Canadian mythos of adaptation and acculturation to the land while transforming its terms. As not only temperaments collide within its walls but also languages, or culinary regimes, mythical tales of Japan, and North American prosaic rationalism, Goto's version of the Canadian West and the imaginative forms of its search for origins indeed begins to resemble a house of "f(r)ictions".

When a Man's Gotta Do...

Although, as I have already maintained, there is no integral, unified vision produced in the novel but rather the tracing of historical, social and personal disjunctions and their difficult resolutions, these discontinuities in turn provide a critique of the iconic representation of the prairie as: "Masculine. Manly. Virile", to quote van Herk (1992, 139). The interweaving of folk tale, Japanese myth and realism in the narrative serves to remap epistemological and social territory. Similarly, travel itself, the signifying domain of that prairie man/horse tandem, becomes feminine tale when Naoe sets out from the house on foot into the snow to literally "inscribe" the Western territory. As she leaves in order to "walk and sing and laugh and shout" (Goto 1994, 108) across the country, she reappropriates strategic spaces of cultural mythology for other imaginary ends. As she takes on the "indifferent" prairie (van Herk 1992, 139), a "landscape ... garrisoned by the art that represents it" (141-2), the image of man alone against the land is chal-

lenged. The metaphorical perspective on a prairie landscape of representations as one "without entrance ... only imposition, juxtaposition"
(141-2), as a vantage point of "description, and more description"
(141), is rewritten. Furthermore, the incongruity of an old Japanese
woman, suddenly become youthful, travelling with a Canadian cowboy who speaks Japanese, presents an unfamiliar combination of elements that serve to highlight stereotypes and playfully question their
limits. Through the incongruous meeting of such opposites in the narrative, difference(s) therefore foreclose(s) any attempt to contain experience within a single version. As Mary Condé points out, with
regard to the grandmother's trickster-like transformations, at such
moments the narrative "operates on the border between social realism
and fantasy" (Condé 2001, 135).

Yet the re-evaluations that are undertaken in the narrative are not
only directed towards Canadian cultural myths. They challenge perceptual limitations on both sides of the border. For Naoe, enclosed in
a linguistic and perceptual past resisting all influence from her sur-
roundings, is likewise transformed. When she hitches a lift with the
cowboy, they in fact take off on a journey towards a more general re-
evaluation of the stereotyped "Other" through each other; since, when
Naoe detects a "cowboy western drawl" (Goto 1994, 119) where there
is none, when she does not "hear" the Japanese he has been speaking,
her misconceptions underline our propensity to reduce the culturally
unfamiliar to stereotype. The scene, of course, underlines the type of
clichéd perceptions and containment which are usually aimed at the
ethnic "Other" Thus the question of how we perceive difference is
raised, but the very incongruity of the scene, and the inversion of
terms it proposes, prevent the reinstating of value judgements and
dismiss any prejudice on either one side or the other. As the way we
judge each other is held up to scrutiny, and fixed categories are undermined, the narrative shifts cultural and personal goal-posts. Instead
of the discursive "vantage point" on the prairie/nation, as a teleological history of nostalgia for the missing Father, we have a feminine-
centred "insistent, simultaneous, nonsynchronous process characterized by multiple locations" (Mohanty cited in Blunt and Rose 1994,
7).

The grandmother indeed mobilizes several perspectives on subjecthood, since she is situated on several "stages" of being at once; as
troublesome old lady in her daughter's narrative, as storyteller and
mythmaker, as transformative agent becoming the mysterious cowboy
Purple of the Calgary Stampede at the end of the narrative. She is
thus, through her multiple "stages" (in both senses of the word), repre-

sented both as passive object of her daughter's unwilling care and desiring subject, embracing both the body of the cowboy she takes off with and the myth of the "Cowboy" as icon of the West when she takes it on herself. As such she "plunges into" the West, rubs against its codes and categories and abandons the "garrison" to the literary archives. Through this confrontation with the West and this "translation" into the West, (when, becoming a rodeo rider herself, she adopts its guises as disguise), personal subjectivity and national subjecthood become part of a chain of slippery signifiers merging into one another. When she leaps into mythic space at the Calgary stampede, subject and object, reality and fantasy merge in a poetic description: "That smooth clear space where the animal and I are pure as light as sound ... The glide of the animal in your heart and in your lungs and the very blood of your body" (Goto 1994, 219). Not only is the grandmother liberated from the constraints of age and tradition but the text is liberated from the constraints of realistic form.

Reshaping the Self, Reimagining History

If *Chorus of Mushrooms* plays with literary and cultural representations it also challenges a relation of past to present which seeks to represent genealogical continuity as immuable tradition. Through her guise as shape-changing trickster and as picara adventurer, the grandmother upsets both family tradition and the rules of "proper" conduct, thus transgressing the boundaries of social conformity. When she disappears into the Alberta night after years of performing as the mumbling, ill-adapted family heirloom, parked in the corridor as antechamber to the hereafter, she refuses the logic whereby the elderly are merely the past incarnated. She instead offers a revisionary perspective on the displacements and suffering that are the subtext of Japanese-Canadian history. Just as her central role as adventuress in the narrative shifts the traditionally represented role of women from "the house" to "the horse", it also recontextualizes the conformity and discretion which maintain the status quo in the interest of assimilation at all costs, a status quo which relegates to silence the trauma of history and the Canadian responsibility in such history. As Keibo Oiwa remarks: "I believe the whole Nikkei history in Canada continues to revolve around the wartime experience of uprooting, incarceration and dispersal. ... After the war, when assimilation ... became the slogan of the day, the Japanese language went 'underground' so to speak" (Oiwa 1991, 18).

The dismantling of the codes of propriety and silence which the grandmother instigates by her unruly behaviour operates new connections in the narrative, and activates metaphors for the recovery of subjective agency, or "Asiancy" as Roy Miki has termed it (1998, 101). (In this context Miki has taken Atwood to task for her "unqualified erasure of Canadians of Japanese ancestry [by paying] no attention whatsoever to the specific 'Canadian predicament' of their uprooting, dispossession, even deportation, as the direct consequence of xenophic Canadian policy" in her critical study *Survival*).

Thus the subjective shaping of locations which the novel foregrounds is both an answering back to the fate of the Japanese-Canadians – those interned during the war, and those like Naoe who lived through it in Japan – and a reconfiguring of that particular history (or of those particular histories), within in a Canadian national identity. As such, the grandmother's actions and playful antics bridge the gap between "fitting into" the landscape at all costs, and devising a shape to fit a self caught between contradictory realities. Like *Obasan* before, the novel can be seen as continuing the textual reparation of the torn fabric of community which Japanese-Canadian history produced.

Enabling Spaces, Border Crossings

According to Roy Miki, speaking on the difficulty of writing out of gender/racial subjective erasure, the effort to come to voice as a Japanese-Canadian writer has made crucial the claim for a space of Canadian-Asian artistic enablement. This would be a "shifting" space of "vertiginous pluralities" (Miki 1998, 113), as a way of "exploring variations in form that undermine aesthetic norms". It would be one intent on "challenging homogenizing political systems, and articulating subjectivities that emerge from beleaguered communities" (118).

Goto's narrative space does promote such an enabling and shifting exploration into alternative expressions of subjectivity. Her poetics seeks to adequately express the reality of loss, and the difficulty of speech, when the split between worlds and between languages means no one discursive medium adequately reflects the experience of displacement. In particular, since language itself reconstitutes fixed presence, assimilation means not only suppressing the native language, but instating the relation of dominant to dominated that language promotes. This problem of a linguistic split in which the subject is effectively "Othered" within the self as well as in the adopted society is brought forward in the characters' exclusive choice of one language at the expense of the other.

Yet, on another less realistic level, the narrative subverts such a psychic division. As the absent grandmother emerges in the granddaughter Murasaki's mind-space to converse and give advice, the female centres of voice defy rules of consciousness, and the hermetic boundaries of individual (and Western, individualistic) identity are breached. Instead of maintaining the conventions of a realistic, authoritative source of voice, reinstating fixed presence, the narrative becomes a fluid, mobile space where female subjectivities merge, as meaning is "carried across", unmediated by the rational abstractions of the *cogito*. This breaking down of fixed boundaries which allows for the emergence of a collective, heterogeneous identity as an expression of an alternative form of subjectivity is not a mere question of aesthetics. As Miki suggests, such choices are expressions of cultural differences, underlining the links between language and the "homogenizing political systems" he speaks of. When the Canadian cowboy Tengu questions the limits of Naoe's identity, asking: "So, who is Murasaki and who is Purple?" she replies: "The words are different, but in translation, they come together". "So you're a translation of Murasaki and Murasaki is a translation of you?" he continues (Goto 1994, 174). This is one instance of many when the narrative promotes transition, a semantic "migrancy" between distinct ontologies which creates an aesthetic and epistemic opening onto the experience of historical and personal migrancy .

Such discursive strategies are synonymous with the cross-cultural experience of migrancy itself as both discontinuous and synchronous, bringing distinct and often conflictual cultures and histories together with the subject's individual experience. Stressing the liminal and discursive space of such experience, the narrative's unmediated switching back and forth between centres of consciousness, between real event and myth, between past and present, envisages a way out of the oppositional Japanese/Canadian dilemma in which the characters are trapped.

Moreover, as the narrative shifts from one domain of meaning to another, it metaphorically re-enacts the displacement of the Japanese community both within Japan and Canada, thus imaginatively recomposing a fractured community body. For the links made between Naoe, having to "leave again, again, always leaving" (50) in the war years in Japan, and the other experiential spaces in the narrative, set up a network centred in language itself. Similarly, the experience of her daughter Keiko, as she erases her Japanese heritage in order to assimilate into the Albertan population, and that of Murasaki caught between the parents' decision to "put Japan behind [them] and fit more smoothly with the crowd (207)", are moulded in a logic of displacement. By shaping the story in multiple ways, and making story-telling itself central to the conceptual shaping of a viable subjecthood, *Chorus of Mushrooms* thus elaborates feminine "[s]ituated knowledges" (Blunt and Rose 1994, 14), ones which to my mind diverge from the motivating "concern with myths of origin" which Robert Kroetsch sees as the driving force of Canadian literature. For such "origins" (1983, 76), however deconstructively envisaged, posit an authentic narrative of prairie Canadianness as a source which, in his words: "points us back to our own landscape, our recent ancestors, and the characteristic expressions and modes of our own speech" (76). It is precisely the situating of this authentic "own" which is problematical for those whose interests do not coincide with any single image or landscape, whose "authenticity" is invented between cultures rather than within them. *Chorus of Mushrooms* gestures towards a historical and personal "situatedness", but one which makes no attempt to construct a coherent narrative of origins. Instead the female subjectivity which emerges in the novel is sited within multiple discourses, and within those cultural accommodations which hybrid identities necessarily embrace.

Codes of Language: Embodying Cultural Difference

One of the ways such a multiplicity inhabits the narrative and allows difference to emerge is in the juxtaposition of Japanese and English scripts and speech, as the narrative is frequently subject to incursions from the other language, which stops the (English-speaking) reader in his/her tracks.

One effect of the language-mixing is to confront us with what Miki has termed a "baffled textual screen"; a "screen" which, according to Miki (who is using Deleuze and Guattari's concept of "deterritorialisation" here), is "characteristic of minority writing in its interface with dominant society" (1998, 117). We, the readers, are effectively "Othered" confronted with alterity, but in a code which would be legible for Japanese speakers. We are thus put in the "outsider" position. Such strategies therefore implicitly challenge the way we filter reality through binary perceptions of "us" and "them".

Another result of code-mixing is to confront us with thresholds which actively structure difference as a textual effect, and gesture towards possible sites of enablement. One instance is when Naoe recounts the horrors of war, an account which stops at the moment when her father, having spent years building bridges which finally served "the marching steps of thousands ... of Japanese soldiers" (Goto 1994, 47), and too weak to flee Peking, takes leave of them for the last time. Here the narrative stops in its tracks as codes of language switch. This threshold opens onto the unspeakable reality of loss as that which distances the reader, leaving him/her on the (uncomprehending) out-side. But it also registers the very play of inside and outside as that of consciousness itself, structured through language as difference. Per-sonal loss thus opens onto alternative sites of subjectivity; difference becomes enablement.

Antoine Compagnon calls such transplantation of language both a "re-enunciation" and a "denunciation", it focusses on the acts of cut-ting, transplantation and revision (1979, 55, translation mine). The linguistic migrancy at work in *Chorus of Mushrooms* foregrounds cultural difference, and also underlines the dilemma of subjective erasure to the ends of "fitting in": the necessary adoption of unified world views where personal and the public perceptions do not neces-sarily coincide. Yet, such juxtaposition of Japanese and English sites of speech – the displacing from one linguistic system to another – not only underlines difference but establishes "a bridge" (56), a relation-ship between two distinct systems which could be seen as a revision-ary possibility. This hybridity combines two distinct cultural discourses and histories and thus creates a third possibility. As W.D. Ashcroft has stated, the "distinctive act of the cross-cultural text is to inscribe *difference* and *absence* as a corollary of that identity", locat-ing an "aphasic cultural gulf" at the centre of the narrative's workings, one which "remains the energising centre of postcolonial writing" (1989, 71-2).

The other strategy of transplantation in the narrative, the insertion of other types of texts – for shopping lists, newspaper cuttings and a replica of a postcard also litter the narrative – overtly questions the status of master narratives of history and how reality is shaped through inclusions and exclusions, through partial, ideological per-pectives. When various newspaper cuttings give supposedly popular views on "multicultural" affairs, and in particular on Japanese "inte-gration" in the Albertan community, such inserts result in a herme-neutic as well as in a formal disruption as the distinction between history and fiction is blurred.

In fact the cuttings, taken out of their normal context, highlight their ideological positioning and serve in Goto's text to ironize the way the ethnic other is recuperated and "managed" within mainstream discourse. Implicit links are made with the Canadian liberal discourse which deploys "'multiculturalism' ... to project a political and cultural history built on 'tolerance' and 'inclusiveness'". As Miki explains further: "The Canadian take on 'multiculturalism' needs to be read as a contradictory zone of vested interests, ... While its more benign face has supported cultural 'diversity' and 'pluralism', the company it keeps with hierarchically structured relations of "difference" exposes a subtext of racism" (Miki 1998, 211).

The act of decontextualising and reframing bits of text serves to create an ironic distancing and underlines the fact that all writing is *heteroglossia*, that, as Bakhtin theorized, cultural and linguistic difference is at the core of all discourse (see Bakhtin 1981, 259-423). All writing involves moulding separate and discontinuous elements into a continuous and coherent whole as in fact, "... all writing is collage and gloss, quotation and commentary" (Compagnon 1979, 55). The fragments and traces taken from other sources therefore underline the impure origins of all texts and the textual source of all forms of supposedly stable identity, underline the constructedness of narratives of the nation. When the narrative confronts us with a shopping list in Japanese our systems of understanding are short-circuited although we recognize those codes of the everyday which are common to all cultures. We therefore proceed, like tourists in a foreign country, both in partial ignorance and partial comprehension, both in a shared recognition of common cultural codes, the social forms that bind communities together, and yet in a state of in-betweenness where any mastery and subsuming of difference into a stable interpretation is denied us.

Moreover, the iconic quality of such representations as the postcard and the signs designating Asian produce in a supermarket, which are transposed in the text, underline the indicial function of all of the codes we accept as transparent reality. We are reminded of Roland Barthes, who stated in *Mythologies*, his work on the systems of cultural signs which surround us: "I wanted to track down, in the decorative display of *what-goes-without-saying*, the ideological abuse which, in my view, is hidden there" (1973, 11). Just as pictorial representation relies on the faculty it exercises "to show, in order to persuade" (Dubois cited in LeBlanc 1993, 201, translation mine), it points to the arbitrary and partial nature of this "showing", its reliance on all the things we take for granted and the means used to visually incite us to make judgements. While the signs in a supermarket with "Loo Bok", "Suey Choy" or "Japanese Eggplants" (Goto 1994, 91-2) create arbitrary identities regarding the Canadian choice in naming unfamiliar foods, they underline the arbitrariness of all naming. As the scene plays on the strategies of representation governed by seeing and naming, it foregrounds how different categories are created in culture, and the positionings behind those differences and divisions. This chain of differences that the strategies set in motion in the novel therefore demonstrates how discourse – linguistic and by extension cultural – sets up categories as normative devices. But such strategies also multiply boundaries in order to destabilize these categories.

Speaking in Tongues, Speaking Collectively

Braidotti has theorized the female subject as "molecular, nomadic, and multiple" (1994, 171). Stressing the historical conditions of where one is located and the "process of becoming-subject" (158), her work on what could be called a feminine "embodied multiplicity" seems particularly relevant to the forms of subjectivity which emerge in *Chorus of Mushrooms*. For, if the novel sheds light on the way language problematizes postcolonial identity, it equally envisages the particular forms of a feminine, non-hierarchized, collective identity.

Just as there is emphasis on the fluid boundaries of language, storytelling is at the core of the novel's strategies of collective identity-making. The links between grandmother and grand-daughter are made explicit in the play on naming in the narrative. For if Naoe renames herself "Purple" when she leaves home, the latter is the meaning (in Japanese), of "Murasaki", itself a translation (subversively invented by the grandmother), of the English "Muriel", the name which the parents adopt for their daughter. Further traces in the narrative tie "Purple" to the daughter, and "Murasaki" also stands for the feminine creative literary act itself, since we are told it refers to a tenth-century female Japanese writer, "the first person to write a novel" (Goto 1994, 165). Naming in its normal guise, as the most potent element of individual identity-making, is thus here the means to establishing a shared space of identity.

Similarly, as Naoe's tales are carried on, they are both "translated" from one feminine site to another, and the stories become community ones. They participate in the language-shaping and shaping-through-language process which informs the narrative as a whole. As when: Murasaki's "mouth opened of its own accord and words fell from [her] tongue like treasure ... [t]hey swelled and eddied. The words swept outside to be tugged and tossed by the prairie-shaping wind" (21). Just as Naoe sets out on foot to literally reinscribe the prairie, her steps a metonymic shift in a chain of meaning, (recalling once again Aritha van Herk's *No Fixed Address* and her reinvention of prairie space), so Murasaki's words are a protean form, reinvesting prairie space with new signification. We are reminded of Dionne Brand's poetics which seek to recover the collective body of Caribbean suffering through the reshaping capacities of language. Goto's context is, of course, very different, but the strategies of healing the silence of history through metaphors which bypass linear form is similar. That the act of speaking rather than language as meaning is expressed here – the subjective, oral presence rather than the objective pole of communication – finds a corollary in the grandmother's constant mutterings in Japanese, which are described as "words that come from our ears, our mouths, they collide in the space between us" (4). This is the type of heterogeneous babble of words evoked by Barthes as he sat in a bar in Tangiers and listened to the foreign language around him, to the "words, tiny phrases, bits of sentences" which, as they traversed his consciousness, made of him a "souk" (1973, 79, translation mine). The image of the self as a place of cultural, linguistic exchange, (a "souk"), aptly expresses the labile use of language in *Chorus of Mushrooms*.

All these strategies pertaining to voice and subjecthood partake in what could be called a process of disidentification. For they disrupt those links between logical discourse and a coherent sense of self. By constantly confounding the types of connections we are accustomed to make, and inventing others, *Chorus of Mushrooms* underlines the collusion between systems of meaning and identity. When the usual links we make between the faculties of speech, silence and hearing, or between material and abstract qualities are disrupted, the arbitrary nature of such logical distinctions is underlined. Words which "swell and soften" or "flake and wither" (Goto 1994, 18), Naoe's capacity to "smell-taste" (37) her daughter's day at work, all stress the materiality of language. The breaks in continuity between areas of thought, the typographical blanks, the apparent non-congruity between juxtaposed statements are characteristics of such disidentification; seemingly random associations are made which, however, become meaningful when connected to further associations. The way the narrative as a whole privileges the signifier over the signified, the poetic over the systemic gives us an English-Canadian linguistic and cultural space which is reimagined; those Canadian, Western narratives of "the house" and "the horse" are recontextualized.

You Are What You Eat

If language is the space of personal and collective revision and is rendered material, food on the other hand, signifies as a cultural index, as a type of language in the novel. Much like Suzette Mayr's *The Widows*, *Chorus of Mushrooms* seeks, through the inscribing of nourishment as nurture, access to the sensory, bodily foundations of subjecthood itself, access to the way that food not only reflects one's roots and cultural preferences, but also inflects the Self within a specific version of identity. For to eat or not to eat Japanese is synonymous in the novel with the recognition or non-recognition of cultural heritage, but it also renders problematical the question of the seemingly rigid borders which separate heritages. Just as the grandmother and granddaughter surreptitiously share the "crackers dipped in soya sauce, ... and flat leather sea squid" (16) that Naoe has sent over in secret – forbidden fruit that is affectively linked to the grandmother's storytelling – so the daughter's "forgetting" the language goes together with her deliberately renouncing the taste of Japanese food. In a vital way you "are what you eat" here. The codes invested in taste signal an inclusion in, or exclusion from either of the cultural domains which are kept separate for fear of contamination. Just as the grandmother eats Japanese food and refuses to speak English, so her daughter eats Canadian food and refuses everything Japanese; her husband Sam, however, eats and speaks Japanese under cover, (although a peculiar "cultural amnesia" means he can only read Japanese and no longer speak it). Murasaki on the other hand, eats and learns Japanese surreptitiously. Japanese is thus a clandestine traveller in the narrative, the dangerous supplement that could upset the Canadian assimilation process. Moreover the sign that breaches are finally closing in the family is when they all sit down and eat "Tonkatsu", their namesake, and the only Japanese word which Sam can remember, in an act which significantly seals the link between food and identity. This symbolically reassembles the family's identity within traditional custom. As Mark Libin has perceptively remarked: "the word *tonkatsu* becomes a compulsively repeated token of loss and the lever with which Muriel is able to recover her forgotten language and the abandoned route to a Japanese community" (1999, 124).

As such, I would agree with Guy Beauregard (who takes issue with Maria N. Ng's view) that the critique of Asian Canadian writing as "still riddled with the stereotypical images of Chinese laundries and chop suey on the menu of Good Luck Cafés" demonstrates its limited scope here (1999, 71-2, footnote 21). It seems to me that those conflicted signs of identity are both the markers of subjective location, and a particularly complex set of relations governing the subject's ability to be Japanese-Canadian. The interest of such spaces in *Chorus of Mushrooms*, created by the harnessing of food to identity in a performative way, is that they investigate both the limits of assimilation politics, and express alternative imaginary configurations. Mark Libin convincingly analyses the relevance of "smell-taste" as "a grammar" which "reflects an encoded desire to represent sensory perceptions in an immediate and unmediated writing style" which, as he demonstrates, places the supposedly stereotypical "chop-suey" representation at the core of Goto's resistance poetics (Libin 199, 131). This is therefore, to my mind, not "chop suey" writing but a feminine resistance poetics, the novel's pondering on culture both as historically situated and imaginatively reconstructive. It is a working of the interstices of representation, where: "The necessary tie to community establishes that ethnically specific tension of inside and outside that Japanese Canadians have continued to inhabit as a matter of course" (Miki 1998, 110).

Through the linguistic and poetic strategies deployed, the novel thus implicitly challenges the "politics of inclusiveness" that masks the tensions and erasures vehicled by cultural migration itself. It also avoids falling back into an alternative "master narrative" which would reiterate the erasures which have constituted the Canadian-Japanese experience. The incongruity of mushrooms in chorus, matching the incongruity of an elderly Japanese rodeo rider with a Japanese-speaking cowboy scholar, is the novel's response to the inside/outside dialectic which haunts unitary identity formations. The placing of language at the centre of such revision is a way of imagining alternative versions of both female and cross-cultural subjecthood.

Anne Michaels, *Fugitive Pieces*: Geo-Logical Retrievals

> One can look deeply for meaning or one can invent it (Michaels 1997, 24).

Fugitive Pieces, in its own way, approaches history's silencing of community voice. But here it is not so much a question of a state of "in-betweenness" – on the linguistic and cultural border between worlds – as an entrapment in the "unsayable" of history. The dialogue with history that the novel offers investigates the seams of representation where language fails; where community suffering is so radical and all-encompassing that experience seems to split off from its discursive representation. If the hybrid, insider/outsider position elaborated in Goto's work tends towards imaginary revision and alternative subjectivities, *Fugitive Pieces* searches out elusive traces of personal memory through which to remember and re-member a collective, Jewish consciousness. This is therefore not the difficult negotiating of subject positions of *Chorus of Mushrooms*, but the problem of re-trieving, from the trauma of the past, a discursive positioning from which subjecthood itself could be envisaged.

Yet, given the fact that *Fugitive Pieces*, unlike the other works in-cluded in this volume, is narrated through the point of view of male characters, one could ask to what extent the novel elaborates or fore-grounds a female subjectivity. Historiographic fiction has undoubtedly become, in recent years, an imaginative choice for many male Cana-dian writers – one thinks spontaneously of Timothy Findley, Michael Ondaatje or Rudy Wiebe. Ondaatje's *In the Skin of a Lion*, like *Fugitive Pieces*, investigates subjective spaces; it does so through a tech-nique of postmodern collage rendering the immigrant experience during the construction of Toronto. Wiebe's *A Discovery of Strangers* relates the Franklin expedition's encounter with the Yellowknife tribe and much of the narrative exposes the point of view of a female char-acter named Greenstockings. Nonetheless, while it is very difficult, and also inadvisable, to make blanket, prescriptive statements about what constitutes male or female-centred writing, the links to be found within the diverse creative productions in this volume, including *Fu-gitive Pieces*, are those announced in the introduction. The preoccu-pation with psychic/symbolic spaces and their limits, with the relation of language to both an intimate perception of self and social represen-tions remains, to my mind, the central premise from which such fe-male-centred fictions evolve. *Fugitive Pieces* is no exception since, as Méira Cook states, the novel is "a sustained exploration of memory" where the character Jakob writes "to achieve subject-hood" (2000, 13, 15). Significantly, (as I examine later), although the narrative focusses strongly on scientific domains of knowledge, it does so not to elabo-rate a thesis on the cause of the Holocaust but to shift causality itself from its moorings. Subjective memory and scientific rational inquiry are manipulated in the interests of thresholds where one merges into the other; the boundaries between inner pyschic and outer material spaces are constantly questioned.

By contrast, *In the Skin of a Lion*, despite its generic scrambling, elaborates a character's quest for origins involving the search for, and final confrontation with, the capitalist boss Harris, just as it involves the search for another enigmatic figure, Small. The narrative as a whole, although fractured in its structure, is thus, to my mind, deeply informed by this linear and metaphysical quest for the the "father" as both source and continuity. A final catharsis is achieved through the central character's recognition, if not apparent respect for, the (oedipal) structures of authority. Ghosting the narrative therefore, despite the questioning of singular versions of the self or history, is the script whereby Patrick quests to be written into a viable, masculine genealogy. His search for Small and his confrontation with Harris are part of his need to make sense of his destiny; his "identity" therefore depends on seeking, finding, and aligning himself with "his" specific "truth" in the natural order of things. His "meaning" is achieved through recognition (by the "father"), and relevance (to history as the "big story" with metaphysical "truth" as the fixed reference).

Likewise in *A Discovery of Strangers* although the themes deal with the rewriting of history and the redressing of the Canadian native peoples' part in that history, one still has the sense that the inscribing of difference – the perceptions of "Greenstockings" and her tribe – are filtered through a view which is in constant relation to, and therefore somehow legitimized by, the imperialistic assumptions of the colonising expedition the narrative undermines. The British colonial figures of abusive authority are examined in all their misguided arrogance but I am not sure that the symbolic/discursive underpinnings of authority itself is central to the novel's preoccupations. The confrontation between two irreconcilable world views – through which the native one comes to seem rather idealized – does not question the premises of heroism, nor the metaphysical source of "big stories" and their expectations of catharsis. History, despite its violence and misdoings, remains the referential point of invocation, its capacity to confer truth and value is not really challenged.

This is of course an extremely scrappy appraisal of two excellent novels and judging their aesthetic value is not my object here. My point is that the subjective relation to history in these historiographic fictions involves, despite their subversive drive, fixed points of reference which could be called "truth", "recognition" or "filiation". Such points of reference remain curiously intact at the close, reconstructed nostalgically as a point of origin from the very subversive strategies which they generate. By contrast *Fugitive Pieces*, in my opinion, takes as its starting-point the very logic of causality which renders the Holocaust "unspeakable", while privileging, through the examination of individual and collective memory, the paradoxical reconstitution of that "unspeakable" past within language. Perception itself thus remains central to the narrative, and history returns constantly to its own source in language and to its structuring of the subject, not to a fixed point of metaphysical "truth". The cultural transmission of silence with which the narrative wrestles – the rent in both collective and personal consciousness which the Holocaust engendered – does not stand as a transcendent "lack" outside the scope of the narrative's drive. It is rather the problem the narrative sets out to deal with as I hope the coming analysis will demonstrate.

Significantly, the one aspect of *Fugitive Pieces* which is not really convincing, is the love plot. I agree with Cook that the scenes of passion are not moving but sentimental and at times even bordering on cliché, and that the female characters are indeed imbued with both ideal beauty and minds (2000, 17). However, I tend to attribute this more to Michaels' difficulty in adequately rendering scenes of sexuality through the eyes of a male narrator, than to a problem of poetic style. This is a case of narratorial drag, of a supposedly "masculine" voice showing its disguise (its authorial petticoats so to speak) in its recourse to stock phrases and perceptions which are attributed to "masculine" perceptions.

But the novel as a whole, like all the other women's fictions examined, works at, and on, those borders of meaning and perception which inflect and reflect subjective reality. The radical displacements of historical "meanings" which the narrative articulates (and does not reconstruct), the play of voice and threshold, are informed by a relation to social/symbolic meaning itself which is problematical – and which emerges from a female consciousness.

History in Search of a Narrative

The Holocaust still remains the unenviable model of "ethnic cleansing"; it expresses the unacceptable in human terms and remains fundamentally "untouchable" in rational, logical ones. In the sense that, whereas the extermination of the Jewish people occupies a prominent place in European history, it is in some way resistant to historicisation – unable to be accommodated within a rational scheme of cause and effect. For how the "unthinkable" was organized and carried out without opposition within the rigorous framework of the Third Reich organisation, how it was allowed to happen in collusion with not only the German population but other European nations, turns the principles of moral values and rational judgement which legitimize the discourses of Western, liberal humanism on their head. Thus, any examination of the political and ideological motivations is necessarily incomplete, caught up as it is in the social and moral contradictions that enabled Hitler to act according to those same principles of moral value and rational endeavour. As such, as *Fugitive Pieces* insistently demonstrates, the Holocaust marked a crisis of language itself. The Western rational thought governing language and humanism's moral principles in the name of a common good allowed instead those same moral principles to serve the cause of mass annihilation. The imploding of language within its own unstable (because finally partial and ideological) logic – the logic underpinning discourse itself – constitutes the "untouchable" aspect which *Fugitive Pieces* brings to light. The novel interrogates what constitutes the "truth" of personal and community experience, as well as the role of language in the constitution of "truth" in general, as both a reflection and inflection of reality. In some way, the narrative's persistent foregrounding of the way language was an active participant in the Jewish Holocaust posits that the Holocaust was an effect of language. I am of course not stating here that language was a final cause with some kind of immanent machiavellian intent, nor that the Holocaust is to be reduced to mere discursive play, but that Hitler's systematic manipulation of figures of speech to "metaphorize" humans into objects of circulation and distribution relied on the same kind of distancing and abstraction that governs both a liberal exchange economy and discursive systems. According to Jean Baudrillard *"In order to become object of consumption, the object must become sign* ... Today every desire, plan, need, every passion and relation is abstracted (or materialized) as sign and as object to be purchased and consumed" (Baudrillard 1988, 22).

For as an agent of the rationale of extermination conveying an id e-alism which Nazi propaganda used to its own ends, and which it used to displace ethical boundaries, the manipulation of signs served to render material, human extermination abstract, to turn it into an act of substitution in a chain of metaphors. In its concerted search for a discursive position from which to state the reality of the Jewish fate, *Fugitive Pieces* thus investigates the status of language itself. Through the prism of the characters' personal displacement and their attempts to recover a sense of self from the silence of cauterized memory, the narrative ultimately tells the story of what language is unable to say: that of its own implication in ideology, that of its both structuring and mediating of those values it purports merely to reflect.

It is then not surprising that this narrative of "missing pieces" puts the figure of the writer at the forefront of the enterprise to recover the past. The narrative foregrounds the acts of interpretation and creation as a possible "re-figuring" – in the sense of inventing alternative sets of signs – and thematizes this very process. The problem of language and its compromised status is in this way rendered performative, the multiple figures of the writer in the text subverting the fixity which language seeks to establish. In much the same way other women's fictions (for example van Herk's), centre on the narrator's capacity to engender alternative scripts, to reinvent the female self in another discursive guise.

When the two central characters – translator and poet Jakob Beer, and biographer Ben – re-arrange and reconstruct the "fugitive pieces" of family story and personal trauma, they also set about to narrativize history itself, to shape versions of the past through the perspectives of those it had shaped. Whereas Jakob is wrested from a bog in war-torn Poland, beginning his itinerary of recovery via Greece to Toronto, Ben's narrative begins in Toronto, the war-time cataclysm a backdrop to his story. His own research and writing both enmeshes Jakob's within it, and releases the knots of his own ghost-ridden scenarios. As both narratives wrestle with the elisions, secrets, and silences of history's legacy to the survivors of the Holocaust, the two narrator-scribes in their conflated destinies do not so much relate the past as create a textual testimony, one which "gestures beyond itself ... towards a problematical reality which it constructs in the very process of its enunciation" (Oltarzewska 1999, 48-9).

If Oltarzewska's comment on Atwood's *The Handmaid's Tale*, another (but female-centred) historiographic fiction, seems pertinent here it is because both novels centre on the intimate links between selfhood, language and historical reality. Both, in their own way, blur the boundaries between those domains and concentrate on perceptive reshapings. The interweaving of experience and overlapping of subjective spaces within Jakob and Ben's narrative have thus much in common with the narrative/perceptual foci privileged in Brand or Goto's fictions. In all three, as in the other women's writings examined here, reality itself becomes a mediated term, a conceptual framework always under construction.

As a witness to history, *Fugitive Pieces* is an investigation into the capacity of discourse to invent a subject position from which to speak of the unspeakable, to speak of that which apparently lies outside the ethical, moral and experiential boundaries of our knowledge, the means we have to conceptualize and act within the world. The novel is equally an exploration of the relation of such ethical, moral positionings to discourse itself, one which confronts the notion of "unspeakable" as a historical/discursive flaw and which, if it cannot speak of its own experience, informs us instead of the limits of discourse. Jakob and Ben's narratives are efforts at retrieval, at reinvesting the shattered causality of history with meaning, at inventing a way to mourn

the millions that come back to Jakob in sleep as "[t]he grotesque remains of incomplete lives, the embodied complexity of desires eter-
nally denied" (Michaels 1996, 24). The historical "uncloseability" of
the victims' fate thus becomes in the story that of "a problem of writing *after* [which] is also the problem of how to represent the impossible event faithfully while avoiding a betrayal both of history and of
the victim" (Adorno cited in Cook 2000, 12).

Narrative therefore constructs an interface in the novel, situated at
the threshold of silence and subjecthood. A silence which haunts both
narrative accounts and generates a split temporality, echoing the
"double time" of which Holocaust victims themselves speak at length.
"Co-temporality" and "countertime" are concepts which, according to
survivors' testimonies, describe the hermetic time bubbles of "after"
Auschwitz, as they "struggle with the impossible task of making their
recollections of the camp experience coalesce with the rest of their
lives" (Langer 1991, 3). *Fugitive Pieces* wrestles with a similar kind
of fissured temporality (and causality); the characters locked into an
experience which, in its incommensurability, its unsuitability to the
linear unfolding of narrative, refers to "its own historical reality and
nothing more" (48).

As the child Jakob, rescued and taken to Greece by the geologist
Athos, grows up to a world of knowledge, erudition and discovery, he
is effectively caught in the implacable "double time" of trauma victims and his account is only able to evolve by trailing the psychic
debris which precisely impedes such evolution:

> While I hid in the radiant light of Athos's island, thousands suffocated in darkness.
> ... While I was ... learning Greek and English, learning geology, geography and
> poetry, Jews were filling the corners and cracks of Europe, every available space
> (Michaels 1996, 45).

The narrative thus becomes the story of the narrative's impossibility to relate Jakob as subject since language itself, the prerequisite for
subjecthood has floundered, like the Jews from "the ghetto of Hania
(43)", shipwrecked on the cliff-face of humanism's structural lie – that
truth transcends the narratives which articulate its value.

Whereas Athos's stories of Arctic expeditions and geological fracture create a continuity through their projecting of extraordinary logical possibilities, of "bacteria three billion years old" or "fossil
elephants ... found in the Arctic, fossil ferns in Antarctica, fossil rein-
deer in France, fossil musk ox in New York" (30), loss is registered,
not only as a "countertime" but as a "counter-narrative", similar to the
one which Holocaust survivors experience as a lack of "closure, ...

because the victims who have *not* survived ... have left no personal voice behind" (Langer 1991, 21).

Such "evidence that [paradoxically] constantly vanishes" is the tear in representation itself which *Fugitive Pieces* attempts to repare, by constructing a network of relations from other discourses of the human sciences. Such a tear signals the same crisis of meaning as van Herk's search for Ellesmere – a desire to retrieve through language what language disguises. As the fugitive pieces of the characters' past resurface and sink again, referring us constantly to the limits of representation, the discourses of scientific discovery, geology and paleontology provide the narrative's escape from the implacable logic of Nazi teleology: one in which "mass murder ... was not only the technical achievement of an industrial society but also the organisational achievement of a bureaucratic society" (Browning cited in Bauman 1991, 13).

The Geography of Mourning

If Athos's "lyric geology" (Michaels 1996, 209) stages the capacity of human memory and logic to analogize the abomination of the camps, it does so by envisaging the possibility of transmission, by metaphorically folding into rock strata – the earth's memory – the fissured continuity of the survivors' memory. The sealed-off experience of Ben's father, an escapee from the camps in the narrative, leaves him, once free and living in Canada, still inhabiting a "hiding-place, rotted out by grief" (233). Ben inherits this experience as his own particular load of suffering, thereby developing the theme of an impossible mourning in the narrative. Such a "demise writing" develops the "'absent' theme" of the disappearance of others, an "un-story" which "subverts the whole sequence of the [survivor's] existence" (Blanchot cited in Langer 1991, 69). Underpinning such testimonies of the traumatized subject is the necessity of cultural transmission, and the discursive nature of such transmission: not only as access to an acceptable personal history, but as a means to heal the collective, Jewish psyche.

As Jacques Hassoun points out, traumatic events affect the active transmission of culture and personal heritage, turning them into a *"narrative without fiction"*; a successful transmission however, "reintroduces the fiction and allows each person, in each generation, ... to introduce all the variations [allowing him to] appropriate narrative to create his story" (Hassoun 1994, 119, translation mine). One could say that the problem of "transmission", the recovery of agency, and the need to "introduce ... variations" in order to appropriate experience motivates much, if not all women's writing. It is also a particular facet of the postcolonial dilemma since the very history which has to be recovered is that which subjected and enslaved the communities concerned.

In its investigating of novel forms of analogy then, *Fugitive Pieces* is exploring connections which can lead to recovering personal and collective agency, connections which work through redefining the discursive meaning of history itself. By examining what associations can be made which subvert our rational judgements but lie within the realm of human experience, the novel is privileging the personal and the discontinuous over the global and linear. It is thus recentering the focus on history as a reconfiguring, not merely a reassembling, of "fugitive pieces", in order to instigate those discursive variations and creations of which Hassoun speaks, and which constitute subjecthood. The extraordinary events which the narrative relates: "[a] man opens his front door and is carried two hundred feet above the tree-tops, landing unharmed", or "[a] crate of eggs flies five hundred feet and is set down again, not a shell cracked" (Michaels 1996, 224), serves to undermine abstract rational analogy. Universal rules give way to the particular and the local, enunciating the contradictory shaping of personal experience.

When the two narrative accounts overlap, Ben reversing Athos and Jakob's itinerary and leaving Canada for Greece in search of Jakob's missing notebooks, he elucidates the mystery of Jakob's last days, and pieces together his own disrupted personal narrative. Through the search for Jakob's past he finds his own, "retextualized" as a transmission where, through the search for Jakob's life and writings his own life "narrative" recovers its "fiction". The "in-betweenness", so prevalent in the narrative, becomes, as for Brossard's narrator, an exercise in "self-translation".

Rerouting Causality, Rerooting the Self

The film image which is played out over and over again and which seems to emblematize the Nazis' enterprise of logically planned, systematic elimination, is the vision of cattle trucks and railway tracks, the destination part of a complex organisation, its mission a finality of which the "passengers" are uninformed. The teleology of inexorable endings is inscribed in such images, as in the logical term/metaphor "final solution"; that of a master narrative playing out its logic of exclusion and ethnic cleansing to its "proper" end. The unequal balance of power between master planners on one side, and dispersal, hunting down and capture on the other is also expressed in such images. *Fugitive Pieces* is in a way an examination of such a causality, which Western culture made possible: the rigorous and systematic destruction of the ethnic other under the banner of ideals of national identity and honour, those shared precisely by Western culture at large. As such the novel is not limited to a particular period of history, it reaches out to examine the way logic works and the way abstract reasoning erases difference. The manipulation of language and the appropriation of heritage to construct the German narrative of "pure" origins which the novel foregrounds, the way the "cultural storm troops of the Third Reich" (Schama 1995, 81) destroyed Polish heritage because it contradicted this myth, recalls other appropriations, for example that of the Native Peoples' land and heritage in, Canada which the novel itself refers to.

What *Fugitive Pieces* sets out to do is to reroute the logic of the Holocaust and to redirect the silence of history, via metaphor, into the living matter of geology and geography (See Omhovère 2002a, 103-16). It seeks therefore to redeem language through the power of language, to rescue it from the teleology of all unitary narratives of origins and nationhood, and to propose other, alternative sites of meaning.

In the narrative, where abstract causality is inscribed in the literal and the material – the earth's "[r]emote causes" which fascinate Athos, its narrative of both "catastrophe and slow accumulation" (Michaels 1996, 48) – analogies are provided for those for whom time also stopped, but whose encrypting will not provide such perfect artefacts for scientific discovery. If the narrative explores the victims' persistent and insistent vanishings: into the sea off Corfu, into the hills, into mass graves, or like Jakob in the beginning, "hidden like a concealed manuscript behind the wallpaper of the cupboard" (Cook 2000, 14), their presence is however "encoded in air currents and river sediment" (Michaels 1996, 53). The natural sciences allow here, if not the dismantling of the silence of Auschwitz, at least a shift of the terms in which that silence is perceived; the absence of speech of victims it represents signaling a discursive threshold where the language of science meets that of the poetic image.

In his chapter entitled "The Silence of Auschwitz" André Neher identifies three layers of silence: "The camp separated from the world by fog and night, the silence of those who knew and did not speak out, and lastly, the silence of God". (Neher 1970, 154, translation mine)

Athos's descriptions of Scott's expedition to the Antarctic, and that of his archeological retrieval of the "drowned city" of Biskupin, allow for the recovery of the past in the signifying meshes of iconic representation. The pathos of Scott's "arm ... around Wilson and the bag of fossils ... lying next to them", "his frozen men starving in the tent, knowing that an abundance of food waited, inaccessible, only eleven miles away" (Michaels 1996, 36-7), opens scientific discovery onto human suffering. The archeological strata of bodies in mass graves, given to us indirectly through Jewish treasures in the hills – "[a]scrap of lace, a bowl" – seek to transfer and "frame" the "unspeakable", that is, to invent a way of delivering the Holocaust from silence. Yet inversely it also works on those forms of scientific logic – Athos's "[r]emote causes" (48) – which interpret the world through abstraction. The discourses of science are thus put to work to accommodate metaphor. Abstraction becomes the very means of recovering meaning from the *logos*, of subverting and rerouting those logocentric "trains". The Nazis' playing of the "old trick of language, ... [whereby] [h]umans were not being gassed, only 'figuren' so ethics weren't being violated" (165), is played at its own game.

One of the prominent traits of Nazi strategy was precisely their understanding of the power of ethical coercion invested in metaphor, the way it could reconfigure perceptions to accommodate incompatible realities. As the narrator points out, when human beings became "dolls", "wood" or "merchandise" (165), the reprehensible dimension of Nazi practice was effaced through the shift to the figural dimension; when human beings themselves became figures of speech, camp inmates inhabited a world without language, a world of "crushing reality" (Langer 1991, 4). Yet, inversely, the camps' destruction of the distinction between literal and figural divested reality of the symbolic dimension which "makes life real". The renewal of faith that the network of metaphors in *Fugitive Pieces* proposes, by channeling our empathy for the victims through the natural sciences of rocks, riverbeds, air currents and hills, restores precisely the symbolic, discursive nature of the world to its function, by paradoxically filtering it through another genre, through the non-transcendent "Other" of matter. It reasserts for the victims a location as subjects *in* language but not as objects of domination *through* language. The narrative, in its constant deployment of metaphor, thus seeks to create a subjective positioning from which metaphor could, once again, be possible.

Seams of Language, Scars of Memory

Geology and archeology are therefore a kind of representational suture, the dominant themes of discovery and recovery stitching the geological strata – a "reef of memory" (Michaels 1996, 32) – onto the subjective "wounded space" of the narrative. This would be a subjective space occupied by the "ill-come unknown" (Blanchot cited in Langer 1991, 69). Blanchot's term, centering on narrative as a textual space, contiguous with a psychological one, thus blurring limits between outside and inside, shares the conceptual and perceptual focus of theorists of women's place within representation. The epistemological hierarchies and divisions which, as Blunt and Rose's anthology demonstrates at length (1994), are masked by the apparently transparent, separate nature of the world "outside", and represent another type of "wounded" cultural and textual space. *Fugitive Pieces*, as the title implies, makes no attempt at a linear account but deals in disappearance and recovery, cutting across national and epistemological divisions. The ontological suture which the narrative operates on many levels, thus subverts the same presuppositions of mimetic "truth" and singular versions, as do other women's narratives.

Athos's excavating of the bogmen when Jacob himself rises from the mud provides a powerful metaphor linking the logically disparate domains of archeological recovery and mass extermination. As part of "whole cities, under a sky of mud" (Michaels 1996, 49), the bogmen represent a natural cataclysm from another time and by analogy, they speak to the multiple (human) encryptings of the story. As Athos investigates the bogmen's silent world, excavated only to be submerged again in the fervour of Himmler's drive "to conquer history" (104) for the Reich, connections are made between the referential features of landscape and the "genetic features" (48) of lost generations, between the "bogmen's" cataclysmic preservation in "acidic ground" (49) and the Holocaust's traumatic freezing in memory. Moreover, analogies are not only forged across limits of genre but also across those of culture, linking Old and New Worlds in a consciousness which joins both together through its linking of landscape and subject, inner and outer. For the dig in Biskupin is mirrored in the second section of the narrative set in Toronto, "a city built in the bowl of a prehistoric lake" (89). Both cities thus become the "drowned cities" of memory and mourning, their "lakes and primeval forests so long gone they could never be taken away" (102). Subjective perception and objective space are stitched together and geography is grafted onto the scored and scarred surface of personal experience. By providing a frontier, the natural sciences provide textual depth and substance for subjectivity to emerge from alterity. As a threshold of language, one where "[p]uns were a kind of core sample" (100), the fusing of genres thus relocates the fissured narrative of History within subjective perceptions.

If, as Paul Ricoeur says, the semantic shift from the literal to the figurative allows for the opening up of a world, it also extends to "our faculties of empathy" (Ricoeur 1975, 241, translation mine). The jump from Holocaust to rock face thus engages our feelings in a domain where our experiential identification is impossible; since, (as survivors of the Holocaust frequently affirm) the inability of others to fully comprehend the experience is one of the very problems that the sealed-off aspect of that experience reveals.

Narrative Spaces, Subjective Re-Sitings

The analogies which traverse the narrative therefore displace globalizing perspectives and open up localized, subjective spaces within discourse. The narratives of the aborted expedition and the relating of Hurrican Hazel's devastation which uprooted Ben's family for the second time, provide a counter-point to that other cataclysmic upheaval where the "entire street" which "disappeared" (Michaels 1996, 246) can be taken, through the overt reference to Toronto, as a covert synecdoche for a "street full of (Jewish) people" of another time and place. Thus, the Toronto which Athos reveals to Jakob, as he "ripped open cliffs like fresh bread, revealing the ragged geological past" (98), does not evince history but subsumes it within an altered vision, one where the subject is not folded into a universalizing logic, but where subjective experience creates connections. In its privileging of such subjective spaces, *Fugitive Pieces* reappraises those power relations whereby "space was treated as the dead ... the undialectical, the immobile (Foucault cited in Soja 1989, 10". The mobile links which connect disparate domains and disparate cultures serve to reimagine subjective relations themselves. One could say further that Michaels' structuring of such mobile spaces and her collapsing of boundaries links her strategies once again to those of the other women writers examined here. The ability to plunge "one hundred and fifty million years into the dark deciduous silence of the ravines" (98) on Jakob's walks through the city, makes of those cross-cultural geological sites, Biskupin and Toronto, an opening onto subjective resitings, an invitation to re-"place" if not "replace" the traumas of the past in a different connective web/strategy. The continual process of upheaval and change that is foregrounded through the processes of recovery and discovery in the novel is part of such reimaginings in their subjective dimensions. This emphasis on language as process, on metaphor as not just a rhetorical pleasure but as a contentious dynamics links up with Atwood's use of rhetorical play, with her persistent efforts to lay bare what language is unable to express: its own implication in structures of power.

Writing and Cross-Cultural Connections

The conflation of Old and New Worlds, and the characters' individual peregrinations across the globe effect transformations which are encapsulated in the narrative's preoccupation with writing: "The poet moves from life to language, the translator moves from language to life" (109). Changing places allows for the bridging of disparate worlds just as it draws attention to differences; it renders the migrant aspect of travel performative, in that it draws attention both to cultural borders and personal limits. The contiguity and border frictions of disparate domains of knowledge: cultural, personal and linguistic, which the novel foregrounds, become a textual embedding. At the same time cultural differences are thematized as the effect of writing itself.

For the accumulation and diversity of textual artefacts in the novel are part of a general textualisation process in which the character/scribes participate through their cross-cultural/cross-scripting connections. The broadsheet which Jakob finds in Athos' house in Greece – "the Greek translation written in ink under the English, a shadow; the Hebrew translation written above, an emanation" (267) – functions as a sign of the various linguistic and epistemological crossings and recrossings which determine cross-cultural identity itself as discursive enterprise; just as such images signal the importance of texts themselves as reimaginings of identity. The diasporic scatterings obliquely gestured in the earth's rippings and tearings, the migratory characteristics of "massive islands of ice swaying on the sea" (37), also point to migration as a metaphor of the dispossessed Self what Bhabha has called "the unhomeliness – that is the condition of extra-territorial and cross-cultural initiations" (1994, 9). In *Fugitive Pieces* "unhomeliness" seems to signal the condition of cross-cultural reality as a provisional and mobile one, as Athos, Jakob and Ben make of "crossings over" – in their textual, cultural and subjective facets – a mode of reconciliation with the world around them.

Michaels' novel also "relocates" in other ways. When the narrative spans continents it also "re-places" responsibility for the Holocaust.

The latter is revealed to be not a locally contained historical "mistake" but situated within the collective domain, given to a reflection on the part the human race, in its entirety, had to play. Such a re-focussing automatically opens up questions of nationalisms, of ethnicity, and the production of cultural "Others". One thinks of Brand's poetic dynamics, the way her linguistic "crossings" reverberate with particular intensity in the light of the Caribbean history she explores. As in Brand's work, Michaels' grafting of European memory onto New World territory, in particular through the deployment of metaphor as a generic "gate-crasher", serves to invent a type of cross-cultural knowledge, one which fits Graham Huggan's statement on Canadian writing as repeatedly framing culture through both "physical (geographical) maps" and "conceptual (metaphorical) maps" (Huggan 1991, 125). He sees such strategies as a "specific instance of creative revisionism" and a "projection and exploration of new territories", which "correspond to a series of new or revised rhetorical spaces."

Michaels' text can therefore be seen as not only grappling with the "unsayable" of a particular moment in history, but with the impulse to deliver the story of torture of a subjected people into the trans-cultural "text" whereby "kristallnacht" is made to resound through the limestone rifts of Toronto. Thus, in the passage from loss to landscape, from crypt to code, Michaels resites the moral imperative to remember as a transcultural and transdisciplinary project. Moreover she does so within the framework of creative revision which informs all the fictions examined here. The narrative's injunction "not to forget" that which cannot bear remembering, at a time when other massacres, other injustices have rendered "ethnic cleansing" all too familiar, becomes an investigation into possible alternative modes and articulations of meaning. It also examines rhetoric's implication in such "Othering" The embedding of the Holocaust in all the interstices, transformative tensions, energies, and displacements of the narrative works on the notions of "self-presence" and "unity". In its multiple connections across generic borders, it operates through a "rhizomatic" logic whereby, "unlike trees or their roots, the rhizome connects any point with any other point ... It has no beginning or end but always a middle through which it grows and spreads" (Deleuze and Guattari, 1980, 31, translation mine). The traces of the absent, the silenced other and the "Other" as silence itself, are present in every guise in the narrative. At the same time, the mobility and shape-changing of this absent presence, the imaginative investments and displacements at work as graves become molecular or the dead dissolve through pores, confirm the narrator's statement on the strange reversal at work in the active *construction* not *depiction* of memory in landscape: "We long for place; but place itself longs" (Michaels 1996, 53).

By metaphorically rerouting and reinvesting the logic which underlies systems of thought Michaels works at the interface where the subject acts in culture and where culture acts through the subject. Furthermore, by investing the cross-cultural space of Canada and Europe as the means to unsilence Jewish memory and experience – history's "Other" – Michaels operates those border-crossings which continually characterize both women's and Canadian literature in their "Otherness".

For, in its imaginary revisions, *Fugitive Pieces* does not refer back to a structuring self-presence, nor to an absent presence as a kind of transcendent "lack" which could serve to reinvest language with the promise of pristine origins. Instead it is a constant crossing-over between cultural, subjective and generic spaces which seeks to exceed any discursive containment and to produce a literature of encoded difference.

Rough Crossings: Displacements, Destinations and Appropriations

Dionne Brand, *Sans Souci* and *In Another Place, Not Here*: a Poetics of Migrancy.

>...each time I write I find that I've got to go back. I have to go back five hundred years to come back again (Brand 1990, 273).

The multiple displacements of a Caribbean heritage render terms of subjecthood both crucial and problematical in Dionne Brand's writing. Appropriating a personal heritage from within a history of slavery and abuse, while examining and challenging continuing prejudice in Canadian society, implies an exacerbated awareness of the relation of history to the present, and of culture to personal identity.

This chapter aims at dealing with the ways in which cultural displacement, and the effort to reappropriate the past, produce both textual discontinuities and reimaginings. If Suzette Mayr's *The Widows*, examined later in this chapter, does not carry the same weight of anger as Brand's fiction, it nonetheless also investigates the problems of discontinuity and the project of subjective appropriation within a cross-cultural experience. Both novels are concerned with language as the means of reinvention, as a site of hybridity registering the tensions and elisions of subjective in-betweenness. Both conjugate feminine identity and cultural affiliation in a grammar through which identity emerges as a mobile, thus discursive, construct.

Power and Self-Representation

Born in Trinidad and now a "hyphenated" citizen of Canada, Brand, along with other Black, Canadian-Carribean writers like Claire Harris or Marlene Nourbese Philip, challenges the assumption of a seamless integration in Canadian culture on any terms whatsoever. For "Multiculturalism", aimed at accommodating distinct ethnic identities within

the nation state is to her mind a chimera, one which results in relegation to "little cultural groups who have dances and different foods and
Caribana" but which "doesn't address real power" (1990, 274). Thus,
for Brand at least, the in-between space of cultural hybridity is not
easily negotiated. Her status as Canadian-Trinidadian is a conflictual
one as she refuses both multiculturalist pedagogies and the cultural
erasure of an "assimilation".

   "Real power", according to Brand, is inscribed along the dividing
lines of race, gender and class. In this context her own status as a
Black, lesbian, female writer situates her at the margins of multiple
cultural discourses which intersect at a "Centre" defined as White,
heterosexual and phallogocentric. A commitment to political change
has led Brand over the years to work in and for the Black community
in Canada and elsewhere, and to get actively involved in combatting
racism and oppression. It thus stands to reason that her poetry and
prose will reflect this commitment and that writing will become a
social and political responsibility, not just "pure aesthetics" (Brand
1998, 33). Yet she also rejects a didactic stance, one which would
place the writer at a distance, seeing culture "as an object, rather than
from the point of view of the subject" (36).

   The complexity of negotiating subject positions is therefore not
only at the centre of Brand's ethos but of her aesthetics as well. Such
imaginary crossings, to the sites of slavery, to those of African myth,
folklore and revolution, elaborate a poetics through which the distance
of historical time and event is registered as a synchronous, cross-
cultural perception.

   Such a stance towards history is, however, not a nostalgic return to
a lost source but the recognition that the idea of "source" is itself embedded in a nexus of erasure, transformation and deviation, potently
rendered in the image of the "middle passage", with its literal underpinnings in the slave route from Africa to the Caribbean and the
Americas, and its symbolic relevance as a continual displacement of
origins. For an imaginary return means traversing the straits of cultural and racial disappropriation, which is rooted in detour and dispersal. Writing thus becomes a politics expressing experience as "an
instability of cultural signification [through which] the national culture comes to be articulated as a dialectic of various temporalities –
modern colonial, postcolonial, 'native' ... [which are] always contem-
poraneous with the act of recitation" (Bhabha 1990, 303).

   It is, in other words, according to Bhabha, narration itself which
stages the discontinuous reality of the postcolonial subject. Brand
herself designates language as the site where: "the relations of slavery,

of brutality, but also of silence, of distance, of loss ... shape the language I speak" (Brand 1998, 38). Such shaping in turn re-members the mutilated body of an African genealogy, dislocated within the fragmented time/space of colonial history as it was, and is still lived by subjected peoples.

The double movement of a "writing out of" and a "writing in" is therefore particularly crucial to the understanding of the way a historical consciousness informs the cultural imaginary of Black Canadian writing. As Claire Harris states: "I write in a tradition, ... that is in direct descent from European Literature though it clings to what is left of the ancestral cosmos not ripped from me, even as it elaborates Africa in the Americas" (1994, 28).

There are thus no "pure" roots to go back to but instead a project of revision. As Arun Mukherjee postulates, the ironies or gaps informing Brand's poetics are where "African chants, African symbolism, African referents" (1994, 73) dominate, and where, in particular in her poetry, Brand appropriates Western literary forms to "present the oppressive nature of the relationship between Europeans and Africans" (73). Her work uses language strategically, as a wedge to split European traditions, forms and aesthetics apart; to drive them onto their own borders and contradictions.

The notion of a cultural gap rather than a bridge is therefore pertinent here, expressing the discontinuities at work in the fields of time, space and perception. The subject is very much at stake in such writing as it investigates the very possibilities of Black, female self-representation in Canadian cultural space, just it inevitably inflects the contours of such a space.

A Poetics of Fracture: the Self-Divided Migrant Self

In the context of such a politics of representation, the collection of stories *Sans Souci* thematizes the fate of migrants, on the margins of Canadian society, or of poor inhabitants of a perhaps "post" but not "ex" colonial Caribbean. The story "No Rinsed Blue Sky, No Red Flower Fences" juxtaposes an anonymous woman's existence in Toronto's cityscape and a Caribbean "elsewhere" where her children "were growing up far away without her" (Brand 1988, 86). The personal fracture and negation connoted in the title determines the story from the outset, the confrontation between a deferred presence from either subjective location as language fails to adequately register experience. Codes confront each other very starkly in the juxtaposition of the claustrophic spaces of the high-rise flats she transits through, and the imaginary projections of her island "elsewhere". The Canadian "snow white" of the apartments defeats her attempts at injecting col-our into them; the woman herself is in perpetual conflict with the White world around her. An illegal immigrant, she is defined through loss and negation throughout the narrative. With neither a visa nor money, when she has a child this reality too is erased as the child is sent home: "Nor did the baby exist. No papers" (89). In contrast to a Canadian space of the Symbolic, the island "elsewhere" is a fluid economy of flux and desire; the mobile images of "the salt blue and moving water, rushing past her ears and jostling her body" (87), mo-mentarily collapse the rigid boundaries of her Canadian reality. Such images, where subjective perception merges with the landscape in a gesture of renewal, can been linked to the "Rastifarian practice of privileging the 'I' in many words" since such 'i'mages "speak to the essential being of the people" (Philip 1994, 101). Such description then, in its focus on language as a repository of community identity, is pitted against Western, disembodied cultural discourse.

In a narrative where the confrontation of codes inscribes such radi-cal gaps of perception, understanding and knowledge, where inner and outer, personal and public reality do not cohere, the very possibility and conditions of subjective presence itself are challenged. Caught in the double displacement of her own "middle passage" the character's endemic migrant condition is rendered through the description of the woman's "two rooms. Each so that she could leave the other" (Brand 1988, 88). Yet the narrative does not simply oppose an idyllic Carib-bean reality to an untenable Western capitalism. The tourist poster of a "girl in a wet T-shirt, the sea in back, the sun on her body" (89), is shown as yet another discursive displacement, a construction of the island paradise masking the reality of "dry hills back home" (89). Brand is therefore intent on questioning the logic of representation itself, those sets of binary opposites in which Black identity is con-tinually "Othered" But this is also a story about how to fit into the Canadian "vertical mosaic" as a Black person in a Canada, described by Marilyn Dumont as a "colour colony", if one is "the urban pariah, ... surrendered to apartment blocks ... [part of the] survivors of the 'white' noise" (Dumont 1994, 55). This story, as others in the collec-tion *Sans Souci*, thus directly addresses issues of race and class in a country which prides itself on its tolerance. As a nameless exile, the woman in the story is also given no independent narrative voice. Re-duced therefore to the silent space "between worlds", her failure to find a position in either mirrors the narrative form itself in its strategy of gaps and discontinuities, as oppositions are left unresolved. The haunting ringing of a telephone echoing through the empty rooms crystalizes both the woman's increasingly strangled existence, and that of the narrative itself, since it is unable to elaborate a coherent space of subjectivity: a discourse within which the migrant condition could be coherently enunciated. There is seemingly here no opening towards a negotiated, Canadian cultural hybridity, as in Goto's vision; rather a constant desire to find a source within a racial heritage and draw from it a political aesthetics founded in the orality and myth-making of that heritage. Story-telling itself becomes the grounds on which the female subject can be woven into history as "her" story; a symbolic/poetic texture energized through female characters possessing those powers of transformation and magic conferred by the Caribbean/African oral, mythic culture. This presence, located both within community culture and female subjectivity, provides a revisionary focus countering the discursive absence characterizing contact with the White, capitalistic world.

Revising Colonial History: Appropriating a Collective Past

Such a revisionary force is deployed in the "The Lisbon Plate", a first-person narrative set in a bar in Toronto, where many of the patrons are ghosts from the past and the narrative resembles an uncanny dialogue with colonial history. As the narrator journeys through the past at the hands of a "revenge-seeking story-teller magician/witch" (Renk 1999, 98), the colonial panorama opens up and kaleidoscopic images of torture and disappropriation overlap. Within this multi-leveled narrative there are several temporal strands: the narrator's militant present as she comments on the Portugese bar owner Rosa's involvement in neo-colonial doings in "Angola and Mozambique", where, while she "entertained in the European drawing-rooms" (Brand 1988, 96), her brother slaughtered a village population. There is the mythic time of the obeah/harridan as she combs the "Sargasso for bones and suicides" (102), leading the story through the graveyards of colonial slaughter in order to both remember and re-member the traumatized body of Africa. We also have the temporal thread dealing with the narrator's childhood in the Caribbean with her aunt who was later to go mad.

All these narratives interlock and overlap, stitching disparate worlds together while investigating their colonial underpinnings. In doing so they create the kind of texture that is a facet of the trans-cultural Caribbean imaginary: "the fossil spaces of time ... [which] make connections to the families of eclipsed or exterminated native

people" (Renk 1999, 10). Such a syncretic perception is at work here
in the narrative weaving back and forth, registering both the colonial
abuse of the "the money changers and the skin dealers, the whip han-
dlers, the coffle-makers and the boatswain" (Brand 1988, 105) and the
contemporary neo-slavery conditions of the "African labourers [who]
got killed and ... fell to their deaths from third floor police detention
rooms in Johannesburg" (106).

Furthermore the act of story-telling itself is where such conflictual
histories intersect within subjective experience; the narrator's taste for
"telling stories" (99) matches the old harridan who "had stories" (98),
or Elaine, the would-be African princess who "picks up on great stories" (101). All these feminine narratives are one; as Kathleen Renk
states, the witch/storyteller "embodies the voice of the subaltern who
tells the collective story of the lost feminine and slave past while she
comments upon contemporary social conditions that continue past
oppression". The narrative envisages transformation as the harridan
plans revenge for colonial sins, thus enacting an imaginary reversal of
power relations. As the identities of witch and narrator merge, new
forms of community ritual are inscribed, which pitch an African in-
cantation against the "oceans of blood" (114) spent by the slaves.

Such "writing back to the centre" (Rushdie cited in Ashcroft et al.
1989, preface) in its recovery of history thus envisages the retrieval of
a subjective positioning from within the logic of colonialism itself. On
the other hand, the madness of the narrator's aunt in her indelible
blackness, which no "[h]air slicked back to bring out the Spanish and
hide the African can disguise" (100), represents the alienated status of
the subaltern caught up in the debilitating self-representations of an
assimilated "inferiority". The narrative registers the forms of cultural
anxiety which, in the colonial imaginary, were projected onto the "uncontrollable" (because ostensibly dangerously sensual) female, colonial "Other". For, as the unstable signifier "black" circulates in the
text, in the "thick green garden" where "[t]he soil was black", where
the aunt would "grab us, and scrub us as if to take the black out of our
skins" (100), the poetic texture registers the inherently mobile, because constructed, nature of the Black "Other". Moreover, the aunt's
falling into madness and thus out of a "lawful" discourse, is a way to
underline, as well as to re-evaluate, the fantasy of "colony and the
female as ... loci of madness" (Renk 1999, 91). But "The Lisbon
Plate" does not only focus on the disasters of colonialism, it also revises perspectives on a biased, European, literary history, taking Camus' *The Stranger* as its premises, and reviewing the killing of the
Arab in the narrative by seeing it from the perspective of the Arab as

colonial "Other". It thus places racial oppression within the general framework of both colonial and neo-colonial oppression, by stressing European modernist literature's propensity to repeat the erasures and appropriations of it imperialistic past, even as it poses as a literature of Western alienation from such a history. For, as the narrator points out: "Camus works it so that the sun gets into the European's eyes ... But killing an Arab ... is not and never has been an alienating experience for a European. Didn't it ever strike you that Meurseult was a European and the Arab on the beach was an Arab?" (Brand 1988, 111) As Brand deconstructs the primary focus of *L'Etranger*, and then rewrites the scene from the other point of view, she implicitly takes issue with a range of fictions revealing modernism's metaphysical self-questioning while eliding fundamental questions concerning the relation of First to Third Worlds. One could, for example, cite E.M. Forster's *Passage to India*. In her reading of Forster's novel Sara Suleri states that the novel "is characterized by the desire to contain the intangibilities of the East within a Western lucidity, but this gesture of appropriation only partially conceals the obsessive fear that India's fictionality inevitably generates in the writing mind of the West" (Suleri 1987, 107-13). One could also mention Joseph Conrad's *Heart of Darkness* which represents for Bhabha, "the ideal of English civil discourse" (Bhabha 1994, 106-7).

Property and Propriety, Representation in the Father's Domain

Certain stories in this collection deal with the enduring, contemporary neo-colonialism in the Caribbean. They reveal the inequalities of race and class to be integral to the mechanisms of Western capitalist markets in its dealings with the Third World. They also portray such inequalities as still embedded in social, cultural and literary representations themselves. Theorists such as Mukherjee, speaking on such biased cultural representations in Canada itself, have ironically invoked one of the standard images of Canadian nationhood – that of the "[t]he Great White North" – in order to take issue with the national discourses which see colour and not cultural diversity as the criterion of value.

As far as the Caribbean is concerned, as Renk points out, other tropes of representation are at work, like that of the "country estate", which represents the paternalistic hierarchy and projects the Victorian "ideal" family unit as governing principal of purity and moral good onto the Caribbean. As she argues, such representations only served to mask the reality of violence, dispossession and *métissage* which led to the "West Indian color-class system", (Renk 1999, 85) where "White", in all its privileged connotations, became the desirable model. The colonial estate, with its masterful yet morally upright proprietor, the guardian of the paternal Law, is played out abundantly in Victorian fictions where the ideals of property and propriety are vehicled and often prove a source of cultural anxiety. One thinks, for example, of Bertha, Rochester's first wife in *Jane Eyre*, the Caribbean, and thus excessive, feminine, colonial "Other" to Victorian morals who was relegated to the attic. Jean Rhys's celebrated *Wide Sargasso Sea*, which focusses on, and operates a rewriting of the Carribean figure of Bertha, is of course a notable example of the ways in which women writers have investigated the cultural anxieties embedded in such colonial fictions. As such, the Victorian house and the colonial estate, in their hierarchies and suppressions, are metaphors which crystalize the contradictions and tensions inherent in the Victorian model and its complicity with slavery, sexual domination and brutality.

The story "St Mary's Estate" is this model seen from the other side, as the narrator visits the plantation where she grew up, and where her grandfather had been the overseer until he was fired when "age was tired of holding out on his face and when he was unable to create a vision of acres of rich purple cocoa trees for the estate owner" (Brand 1988, 47). The narrative foregrounds the ties of dependency and feudalism governing the plantation world, where the grandfather spent his time and used his strength earning a pittance, "depending on what was not possible, riches, and escaping payment of the debts he incurred dreaming about it" (47). Just as the narrative explores the brutality of plantation life, it also reveals the tenacity of colonial representations, and the lasting damage done to the Black Caribbean psyche. It is also clearly Brand's intention in this story, as in others, to underline the enduring ties of colonialism within contemporary society. For the narrator's reflex when faced again with "the great house" is to obey the "imperative of habit and station [which] causes [her] legs to stand where they are" (49). The house is now abandoned, the slave quarters empty, the narrator is living in a different reality, and yet the assimilation of limits and barriers has endured. It seeps into the very texture of the narrated discourse where a mindless repetition of divisions and boundaries seems to rhetorically perform the conflictual hierarchy: "This is where I was born. This is the white people's house. This is the overseer's shack. Those are the estate workers' barracks. This is where I was born" (49). As language itself becomes stuck in the groove, the split psychic awareness of the colonial legacy is inscribed as a textual configuration. Significantly, as the narrator leaves the scene, that legendary figure of the repressed Victorian imaginary resurfaces, as if emerging from the Caribbean cultural unconscious, within the image of the "picture of the green house in [the narrator's] head, ablaze" (51), thus replaying Bertha's setting light to Rochester's estate, his "house of the Empire".

Myth, Magic and Orality: Speaking the Creole Body

Apart from the dominant "place split and ... time split" (Brand 1998, 31) which deeply inform Brand's fiction, focussing on both dispossession and the reappropriation of the past, her fictions have an intensely poetic dimension, steeped as they are in Creole dialect, expressing how, in Brand's words: "the relations of slavery, of brutality, but also of silence, of distance, ... shape the language that I speak" (38). "[S]yntactic ruptures and localized idioms", indeed inform her poetry and fiction and, "[r]ather than widening the shadow of the 'green oak of English'", undermine the authority conferred by that standard English (Wiens 2000, 83). This orality in her work equally addresses the community body, as shape-shifting mythologies, folklore and magic addresses an Afro-Caribbean cultural heritage.

The figure of the grandmother, one of the central sites of a Caribbean, feminine, Creole consciousness is central to "Photograph. However, the story also foregrounds the conflicted aspect of such matriarchal representations from the point of view of feminist revision. As Denise deCaires Narain points out, critics (including Brand herself) have "stressed the centrality of the woman's body as symbolic fodder in inspiring the colonizing 'mission'", one where "mother tongue and motherland became conflated" as part of a nature/culture dichotomy (Narain 1999, 99). According to deCaires Narain, it is time to "describe and de-scribe" (99) such essentialist representations of women. Yet, as she continues, "writing the body" can be a strategy deployed in the "de-scribing" of such discourses, as an interrogation of the "Othering" of the feminine in representation and language, and also as a tool for the elaboration of an alternative aesthetics.

"Photograph" offers an example of such a "confrontation between texture and the Law" (Smart 1988, 27, translation mine), through its privileging of a community, maternal space in which the grandmother represents the "M'Otherland". Smart deals with feminine representations and textual figures in specifically French-Canadian writing, but her conceptual foundations seem equally relevant to English-speaking women's writing.

Such feminine matrix of imaginary identification, where collective memory takes on a syncretic dimension, also recalls Wilson Harris's concept of the cross-cultural continuum: "the cross-cultural body or bodies of many civilisations whose past, whose traceries, whose elements, whose curious voices ... we are susceptible to" (Harris 1991, 28).

For the grandmother's domain is where magic, language and voice merge, where "her tongue lapping over a new story" combines sensory registers, where the stories spun, or instructions on "how to catch a soucouyant and a lajabless" are integral to her role as storyteller and community consciousness (Brand 1988, 71-2). Using the metaphor of the verandah of a house, "not [as] the surplus of the building but the excess which redefines the building itself" (Ashcroft 1994, 42), such an economy of memory and labile difference in postcolonial discourse represents, according to Bill Ashcroft, "the body, place, language, the house of being itself [which] are all 'verandahs'. That is, they are a process in which the marginal, the excess, is becoming the actual" (42).

In this sense the grandmother can be seen as articulating an altered perception, one through which a heterogeneity of forms sliding between reality and fantasy captures time and place differently. In its emphasis on fluidity and materiality such a subjective site is also the space of the female body and that of writing itself in Hélène Cixous' definition. A body which, in "its infinite and mobile complexity ... with its thousand and one thresholds of ardor" (1981, 256), declines Carribean in the feminine. However, the figure of the grandmother can be compared to that of the mother whose alienated status in the story is radically opposed to the grandmother as "idealized object". As Caroline Rody states, in much Carribean fiction the "middle-generation woman, the heroine's mother", inextricably bound up with the negative image of a colonising "Mother" England, bears the weight of "a pychologically difficult inheritance" (Rody 2001, 121).

If the grandmother in "Photograph" is the site of a feminine, embodied difference through orality and storytelling, other female figures also have the role of transformative agents. Blossom, of the story "Blossom, Priestess of Oya, Goddess of winds, storms and waterfalls", who becomes the magic-making obeah woman, is another avenging presence of slave history, a spiritual freedom fighter, resembling the harridan witch figure of "The Lisbon Plate". When Blossom's bout of madness triggers her transformation into the Goddess Oya, boundaries between the real and the transcendent collapse. Yet, as Renk has underlined, Blossom does not investigate a "'pre-

Columbian' past" but "draw(s) on its New World culture, shaped in part through its African ancestral beliefs in spirit possession, to re-create the postcolonial female subject's vision" (1999, 102).

To this end, the Creole dialect of the narrating mode serves to dis-place a neo-colonial cultural domination. Orality becomes a strategy of re-appropriation when the narrative takes the reader imaginatively back through the "middle passage" to Africa, creating, through the linguistic code-switching, a seam where "the culture affirmed ... as 'indigenous', or 'national', confronts the other as 'imperialist', coloni-alist or 'metropolitan'" (Ashcroft 1989, 71). As the reader crosses the linguistic threshold, and then retreats further towards the African source, to the chant of Oya, the centre of the narrative focus is radi-cally shifted and Africa is implanted at the centre of the dominant "English" code. The narrative effects a revisionary journey back to the past and, as the narrative's discursive practices are destabilized, a cultural interface is created in which the balance of power between linguistic, and thus cultural forms, is modified. Such a revision is therefore not only an imaginary retrieval of the past, but a signifying shift operated within the English-Canadian cultural matrix, as the dominant Anglo-Canadian culture is imaginatively reshaped through a Carribean/African perception.

Moreover, this textual inscription of difference promotes an ex-tremely mobile narrative dynamics. For the language continuum plays along registers from "standard English" to "broad Creole", the narra-tive texture thickening in opacity where the dialect registers most – "It ain't have cuss, Blossom ain't cuss that day" (Brand 1988, 33) – and sliding back to relative transparency at other moments. So language itself partakes of the radical "shape-shifting" going on in the story, as subjectivities merge and distinctions between the natural and super-natural collapse.

Such strategies serve to further challenge the fixity of Western, hegemonic positions. As narratorial presence, Blossom's voice is of-ten indistinguishable from that of Oya, which serves to blur limits between worlds and render indeterminate the source of voice. Yet when the narrator takes on a discrete, "authoritative" identity to relate events, this site is also appropriated by the Creole dialect, thus rein-vesting realism's controlling consciousness by an imaginary "voice of the people". Such subverting of conventions, as Jason Wiens analyses in Brand's poetry, constructs "an enunciative space characterized not so much by a contestational dialogue with a 'standard English' as by 'standard English' utterances themselves that become submerged, appropriated, and placed in a subordinate position" (Wiens 2000, 89).

By imaginatively giving back authority to the community, and by undermining the hierarchy of realistic fictional devices, the narrative surrenders authoritative control, just as the reader is obliged to do. As such, the fundamental "shape-shifting" of modalities of language and form in the story also works on, and revises, the shape of our fixed assumptions and desires as Western consumers. It posits a space where writer, reader and character converge and collude in the effort of reconstruction, thus "breaking down preconceptions, stirring up doubt, rattling judgements, shifting boundaries and unfixing fixities" (Melville cited in Welsh 1999, 146). Brand herself is eminently qualified to express the various modes of "shape-shifting" which have modelled her own existence. Such fictions therefore also address the writer's experience of crossing worlds and confronting the ideologies which inform the relations of power between the Carribean and the West.

When Worlds Meet

If the stories in *Sans Souci* are directed at "shape-shiftings" – revising the colonial past and deconstructing forms of Western neo-colonial domination – Brand's fiction also addresses specific historical moments of crisis to focus on the way global capitalism and Western interventionist politics affect the Third World. Her novel *In Another Place, Not Here* exposes the disparities and conflicts between the West and the Third-world by linking historical movements in North America in the 1960s and 70s to the attempted revolution in Granada. New World economic interests and the exploited Carribean thus meet within a female-centred narrative, against a backdrop of slavery which constantly pressures the text. The antagonistic spaces of "White" and "Black" reality, both in North American and the Caribbean, are examined within the personal accounts of the three women who "attain a kind of allegorical status" in the narrative, in that "their positionings revolve around and through various longings and conflicts that haunted attempts for social transformation" (McCallum and Olbey 1999, 161). Such antagonism makes cultural and personal displacement the central premise of the female characters' reality as shifting from Third to First World does not provide them with a destination, and shifting back again does not provide a sense of belonging. When Verlia, the militant activist, returns to Granada from Canada to participate in the revolution she states: "It's really some colonial shit happening with me. All this fear for a place I should know" (Brand 1997, 206). She thus expresses – as the whole, complex narrative web does – that cultural displacement is a subjective positioning within the hierarchies of discursive, power relations, and not an objective given.

Seen through two narrative focalizers: Elizete, the exploited worker, first in the sugar-cane fields and later as an illegal immigrant in Canada, and Verlia, relating her time in activist groups in Toronto, and her engagement in the "coup" in Granada, the story spins out like a dialogue between women who "ghost" each other's past and present. Together they make up a narrating consciousness which sets out to reconstitute a trans-cultural experience of prejudice and colonialism: Elizete as the submerged, subaltern voice of the Caribbean community defined by her "Who is me to think I is something" (4), Verlia refusing her relations' isolated existence in Sudbury where "the college to study physiotherapy and then the skinny Black man and the house" (150) they wish for her is merely compensation for avoiding "the trouble of their skin" (149). As the narrative voices shift back and forth and the action shifts from North to South, the characters "flights" from one to another are indeed a way of representing "the process of globalisation ... registered in the more material sites of the bodies and psyches of its victims" (McCallum and Olbey 1999, 165). As McCallum and Olbey convincingly demonstrate, Brand confronts the past, not merely to bear witness to a Carribean history of oppression, but "to speak more effectively to contemporary [globalising, transnationalist] forms of oppression and liberation" (165).

The culturally and mythologically potent terms of "landing", "leaping" and "flying", which resonate throughout the narrative, textually rework, through their slippage, such forms of oppression and liberation. For, if Elizete "lands" in Toronto an extensive play on "landed up", "[l]and up", "[l]anded like a fish" (Brand 1997, 46-7) translates her dispossession as she tries desperately to gain "landed immigrant status". The signifier "flight" links into the slave narratives where African folklore of flight and transformation provided "enablement" narratives of escape from captivity, ones which often took concrete form through escape and "flight" to Canada. McCallum and Olbey analyse the doubling of Brand's narrative with the route taken by antebellum slaves to Canada and its utopic dimension at the time, and consequently the ambivalence of this re-enacted trajectory given the negative representation of (unprivileged) immigrant experience in Canada which the novel foregrounds (see 1999, 159-82).

The notion of flight also provides the potent image at the close, when Verlia's fatal leap off the cliff in Granada, in the wake of the U.S. invasion, is not only an admission of the failure of the revolutionary enterprise, but gains a mythological dimension through the grammar of enablement deployed in the dream logic which plays out like an antebellum slave song, in a call and response pattern: "One dreamed she multiplied into pieces and flew away, one dreamed his feet clawed and he flew away, one dreamed he feathered and flew away, one dreamed he sprang like a tree, one dreamed she blew into dust" (243). Such mythic polysemy provides the poetic and political drive of the novel, and, I would postulate, provides a discursive field in which to express the vulnerability which is part of migration: the "landed up" not "landed" status of Elizete. Such poetics are culture as an "enactive enunciatory site ... a process by which objectified others may be turned into subjects of their history and experience" (Bhabha 1994, 178), which goes hand in hand with Brand's project of denunciation and revision. As she creates uncomfortable parallels between slavery, colonialism and global capitalism she creates a syntax which, much like that of Tony Morisson's *Beloved*, echoes with the "visceral contractions" of a diasporic body where the "literal marks on African slave women's bodies have become marks of a literate text, signing the narrative with scars" (Brock 1996, 127). Elizete's scarred body registers the same type of textual inscription, that of a collective body within which "there was no belonging that was singular, no need to store up lineage or count it; all this blood was washed thick and thin, rinsed and rinsed and rubbed and licked and stained" (39).

This is not, however, a mere "metaphorising" of culture (Krishnaswamy cited in McCallum and Olbey 1999, 165-6) as an abstract operation of erasure of cultural memory and suffering, but rather culture as "metaphor" in a very political, ideological sense: that is, as the way in which the tensions, ellisions and displacements of language register the material forces at work in the discourses from which it emerges. (McCallum and Olbey side with Krishnawamy's view when he takes issue with a critical "metaphorisation of postcolonial migrancy which erases the pain and suffering of such migration itself).

It is, to my mind, in Brand's solliciting of the gaps, erasures, and psychic wounds of the past within a dense poetic texture that the drama of colonisation is most pertinently registered as a contemporary trauma of Western civilisation. For such a texture links the events of history to both collective memory and individual consciousness. Moreover, such a poetics establishes links between different domains of knowledge and experience which cut across the logical continuity of history, but can nonetheless be contained within the scope of subjective positionings and perspectives. The historical reality of slavery can not be undone through metaphor but neither is the suffering inherent in such a reality diminished by metaphor. Since language is the repository of symbolic identifications it constitutes the cultural bedrock that both past and present share. It allows for the imagining of alternative spaces of subjectivity which provide angles of visions from which to view and "re-view", and thus challenge, the past from within the present. Language is also the means of linking the abjection of colonisation, in its "unspeakable" aspect, to the present, the only way, in the final analysis, of delivering it from silence.

Suzette Mayr, *The Widows*: Kanada/Canada, Bridging the Gap

> To write the immigrant self is ... to fiction a present and a future out of a self-censored past. We all want to escape our autobiographies and we all insist on reading our best story (van Herk 1991, 187).

If the form of cultural "hyphenation" announced in *The Widows* does not envisage an imaginary retrieval of racial, cultural origins, it nonetheless problematizes cultural and personal displacement. For "self-translation" from one space to another, in this case from Germany to Canada, is shown as entailing its own load of revisions of the past and reinventions. As Claire Omhovère states, "if one set of cultural icons simply came to replace another ... [the characters'] story would be redundant" (Omhovère 2002c, 122). This novel therefore speaks to and from those uneasy accommodations made within both national and personal recitations of identity which accompany cultural relocation.

Subjective Relocations, Narrative Thresholds

As an unlikely story about three elderly German ladies turning their lives around and making a statement on their existence by taking off over the Niagara Falls in a space-age capsule, *The Widows* is a fraught encounter between private grief and public necessity, between old age and desire, between ethnic and social dimensions of identity. The personal dislocations represented by such contradictory realities, serve to highlight the erasures and partial truths underpinning supposedly transparent perceptions of identity itself. Furthermore, the personal negotiations between Canadian and German identities which the novel stages open onto a system of narrative negotiations, one in which the plot itself is caught up in a repetition/rehearsal of identity, where narrative is caught on its own limitations. Cross-cultural, feminine identity thus reveals itself as difference, as a signifying threshold opening onto a discursive space of multiplicity.

For when Hannelore Schmitt negotiates the jump from cemeteries, old family feuds and war memories to Edmonton – "[t]he greatest shopping mall in North America" (Mayr 1998, 15), dragging her reluctant sister Clotilde with her, her cultural jump rehearses that other leap of faith they are to take twenty years later, when they take off over the Niagara Falls. As the sisters set out to visit Hannelore's son Dieter, his wife and their new-born daughter, another personal and cultural dislocation is operated: German funerals as final destinations give way to difficult departures as the new-born daughter already rages against a family tradition by which Hannelore's "father always preferred boys, [and] Hannelore also preferred boys" (9). Thus if, for the elderly Germans, deadends inspire beginnings, since the "three funerals in one day" (38) of life in Germany was one of the reasons given for moving to Canada, beginnings also rewrite endings. The grand-daughter as a new arrival, described "lurching over the precipice" and "barreling out" (18), echoes from the start that jump in a barrel of 1901 when Annie Edson Taylor was the first woman to brave the Falls. Moreover, the links which are made between the two events points to history's repeated tendency to prefer boys. If Cleopatra Maria's birth is the trigger for the sisters' transatlantic move, it also sets in motion other narrative directions and repetitions. When Hannelore, working as an usherette in Edmonton, sees the touring show *Niagara! the Musical*, she not only encounters Annie's great event in tacky remake – "the lit-up miniature Niagara Falls ... with tiny barrels bobbing in the water" (72) – which is to inspire her own dream, but she also makes the acquaintance of Hamish, the lighting man, and his coveted space-ball, marking her own fresh beginning in the domain of "the most disgusting lust possible" (139). Just as she "falls" for the ball, a hi-tech sexy remake of Annie's Victorian barrel, it will enable the pensioners to renew the declaration made a century before: that elderly women are not a useless burden nor a funeral ending waiting to begin. Furthermore, in this narrative of multiple "falls", one suspects Mayr of glancing wryly at that biblical tumble from grace and dwelling on its uncloseable (because repeated incessantly throughout history as the masculine phantasm of woman as either temptress or virgin mother) narrative of origins.

Intricately tied up in both repetition and rehearsal the narrative sets out to foreground, albeit in playful fashion, the inherently discursive nature of identity and the mobile, contradictory value codes at work shaping hybridity. These are forces shaping perspectives on the past as much as on the future within personal stories where "differences cannot be sublated or totalized because past and present 'somehow occupy the same space'" (Taylor cited in Bhabha 1994, 177). Thus, when too much mourning takes the German sisters over to Canada, Germany is not presented as a single cultural frame within which Hannelore, her slightly odd, lesbian sister, the war, privation and a husband lost too early are indelibly glued; instead it becomes part of the textual process of reinvention, the centre of contradictory, changing perspectives, as Hannelore tries out competing versions of the past and the reasons justifying her move away: "because of the wilderness" (42), "because of the coat" (Mayr 1998, 44), "[b]ecause of the funerals" (38). All and none are true. As a threshold of contradictory meanings, Germany becomes a subjective space in which multiple, uncloseable recitations of the female self are performed and overlap. Furthermore, as various, conflicting perspectives on national identity are offered, the alienating Germany of the war existing in the same referential space as the endearing "pans of boiled red cabbage, chicken Schnitzel, firm cheesecake" (89), singular versions and monolithic representations of nationhood are challenged.

Personal dislocation is thus intimately linked to larger issues of national representation, themselves opening onto all sorts of textual limits and renegotiations. When the Bavarian delicatessen in Edmonton run by Frau Schnadelhuber, who "poured coffee like bordello owners were just another kind of horseradish" (43), becomes the place of "home" cooking for Hannelore, the aporia at the centre of displacement itself is foregrounded. The nostalgic yearning for familiar tastes satisfied in a fictional "German" delicatessen in Canada cohabits with the need to avoid Germany itself, since, when reminded that Germany is "far away" Hannelore's view is given as: "[t]hat was the point" (38). Such contradictory values and vision thematize the mobile, discursive aspect of migrancy, but also reveal the unstable, discursive underpinnings of all identities. Such double vision where versions confront each other in the story is then certainly a way to "reveal the incompleteness or falsity of tradition ... [to] raise questions about inheritance" (Howells 1987, 184), in a more general way. The novel's strategies – in their challenging of the concept of fixed identity, and their questioning of where women fit into such ideologies of the nation – thereby ironize official discourses of equality and inclusion. For the contradictions and erasures which prompt the conflicting realities in the story – Annie Taylor claiming to be forty-two instead of sixty-three, Hannelore's simultaneous attraction and repulsion for Hamish, the way "Cleopatra Maria longs for a normal grandmother who is asexual" while "Hannelore longs for a great-grandson from a granddaughter whom she wishes were asexual" (205) – constitute the sort of "ironic paradox" which Linda Hutcheon points out: one through which "our notions of the accepted and acceptable [are driven] into new, liminal spaces, the spaces between meanings" (Hutcheon 1991, 19). Kanada/Canada, as its shifting, hybrid graphic inscription in the narrative implies, becomes itself a split perspective, a discursive space of "Otherness" which allows the sisters to reinvent themselves and reinvent Germany in a more acceptable guise, within the familiar tastes and unburdensome reality of the curious delicatessen. But such a "Kanada" as hybrid sign is equally a subjective site; a feminine version shaped through the sisters "contra-diction"; their speaking out against the uniformity and constraints of old-age. If the lesbian Clotilde, with a cane, her "eyes moist and sagging" (Mayr 1998, 47), her hair "grey and tough like straw, chopped off squarely, too short at the neck" (106), presents a picture that is poles apart from traditional images of seduction and desire, this serves to underline the stereoptypical and reductive constructions of desirability sold to us. At the centre of this tale about women and their contradictory desires is Annie Taylor herself, a women for whom, according to the historian Pierre Berton, "appearances meant a great deal" (cited in Mayr 1998, 13), who was to all intents and purposes a model of Victorian propriety, refusing to wear a short skirt as "unbecoming a woman of refinement" (Rowe cited in Mayr 1998, 191). That this not-so-Victorian lady is herself inscribed in competing discourses of revolt and submission, propriety and disapprobation, and seen, in the narrative, through the visions of three male historians in a "scansion" which "sounds eerily like a sanction" (Omhovère 2002c, 123), points to Mayr's suspicion of globalizing, metanarratives of history, which her reworking of the figure of Annie and her exploit undermines. As a female Victorian daredevil in the land of male adventure and prowess, Annie articulates the ironies inherent in notions of a "new country" which, at least as far as unattractive, financially-dependent women are concerned, is not so "new" after all; within Mayr's deconstructive strategies Annie serves to underline the historians' appropriation of the event, their fitting it into views of the "proper" and "not proper" which she precisely sought to elide by going over the edge of the Falls. She does in fact go "over the edge", escaping the historians' perceptions through Mayr's fragmenting of their partial views in a narrative which exceeds their reach and turns the lens around, rendering them the object of historiographic investigation. Moreover, the "improper" narrative of three old ladies "breaking out" contributes to a "kaleidoscopic vision" (Beautell 2000, 31) of Canadian culture, an unruly, because uncharted,

recitation of ethnic identity which "the offical policy of multiculturalism, and its proposed mosaic structure, cannot contain" (24).

As such, the strategies of "writing back" to a Canadian cultural
imaginary which the narrative deploys elide any simple commodifica-
tion of the old ladies' story, just as the ghosting of Annie's exploit and
its historicized rewriting effect a destabilizing of any "settled" interpretation of her extraordinary feat. Rather, the multiple strands are
engaged in a constant process of narrative destinations and departures
and invoke a "contamination and heterogeneity" (29) as the premises
of hybrid identity which render the narrative as a whole an unclosed
site of new meanings.

Unlikely Pioneers: UnSettling Canadian Narratives of Settlement

The retrieval of a Victorian adventuress as a model for Hannelore's
outrageous scheme is equally evocative of Susanna Moodie and Catherine Parr Trail's nineteenth century, female Canadian settler narratives, themselves rewritings, as they "both shape immigrant
experience in relation to existing fictional models" (Howells 1987,
23). Mayr's heroines could be seen as continuing the line of specifically Canadian feminine "survival" narratives, while ironizing the
genre in her depiction of such unlikely candidates, and in the type of
scepticism of any teleological narrative of "settling" that *The Widows*
presents. For the trio who have survived the war years – Frau
Schnadelhuber as a resistance fighter/driver for a general's wife, for
whom "smuggling of SS plans, ... was nothing but attitude" (Mayr
1998, 92), the others in deprivation and loss – are suitable inheritors
of Annie's particular version of the Canadian survival myth, of her
dream of becoming visible at last, "of shouting [her] presence to the
world" (148). If Hannelore's encounter with the Niagara Falls of
tourist hype is not Moodie's tale of her nineteenth-century encounter
with the Canadian wilderness, she nonetheless transforms and is transformed by the experience, turning it into a narrative of new beginnings. If the rhetoric of the tourist trade is still firmly in place after the
female trio's jump – the "wondrous, monstrous Falls" of Hannelore's
first sighting matching the sublime image at the end in "a beautiful
country" with "outrageously sparkling water" (229) – what has
changed is the place of the heroine in the myth. Unlike Annie Edson
Taylor, who died a pauper after she had "sold too few postcards of
herself on too many corners beside a replica of the barrel" (241), the
heroines of *The Widows* will cash in on the stunt and live to run the
pseudo-German delicatessen. By the end the male adventure stereo-

type has been worked at the seams, and national icons have been wrenched from their ideological moorings to accommodate difference. There is also the suggestion that Kanada/Canada, in its unsettling lack of coherent origins, will always be in the process of being "settled"; as a country of multiple allegiances it will always be in excess of any ideological closure, any myth of nationhood that is more unifying and unitary than the sum of the diverse parts. As the sublime images of the Falls break down within the contradictory German perceptions, Canada emerges as a discourse of the "Other". As Coral Ann Howells has stated in her analysis of Canada's primary self-representation, "wilderness is not only 'geography and geology' but it is also discursively located within the text as the site of dynamic transformations" (Howells 1996, 25). The "wilderness" here has been recuperated as an unstable and hybrid sign, as the iconic vision of Canadianness becomes, through the eyes of the German "Hausfrau" a paradoxical construct: a "bright green old forest and wilderness" but which nonetheless "could do with a cleaning" (Mayr 1998, 20-1). Furthermore, as the female crew steal Hamish's fetish space-ball, to appropriate the masculine adventure narrative, leaving him with "a sad pain under his kilt" (222), they also make an implicit statement about sexual identifications and their place in the construction of naturalized gender roles and perceptions: that, in the end, the only way they find of "grabbing life by the balls" (148), is by stealing one from the gender which possesses them.

Old Ladies at the Carnival: the Textual/Sexual Body

In its challenging of both ethnic and gender representations *The Widows* relies on conventions which belong to the domain of the carnivalesque, inscribing those challenges on the material and cultural site of the body. Carnivalesque inversion structures the narrative, as it begins with the moment of the jump into the Falls and then folds back and forth to different moments in the past and present, punctuated by the historians' account of Annie's venture. Time is convulsive, condensing to the minuted recording of the Niagara exploit or expanding to the "universal truth" time of History. The text itself thus takes on the material aspect of the body and its boundaries. For as the trio travels through the water in the space-ball, with Cleopatra Maria monitoring their route from the shore, the text performs the spatial and temporal disjunctions inherent in the scene as the trio are experiencing it. The text thus mimes body limits between inside and outside, and differentiations between self and other. When both the narrative emanating from Cleopatra Maria's inner consciousness and that of the world inside the ball share page space, but are nonetheless hermetically sealed in their own distinct, non-synchronous linear account, it forces us, the readers, to register both the exigencies of narrative and the transgression of conventions. The material, bodily aspect of language emerges where its naturalized relation to continuity and meaning, and our way of reading, is disrupted. When furthermore, boundaries are then blurred between the two juxtaposed narratives, when the janitor, attempting to dislodge the ball caught in a tunnel under the Falls, puts both the journey and the intra-vessel narrative on hold, the texture of language itself is exposed in its increasingly vexed relation to continuity. The sexuality of textuality is thus foregrounded; the way signifying difference emerges within logical disruption.

Farce and the Feminine

Similarly, food as one of the most potent values and community consensus, but equally as one of the pleasures of the body, comes into play, signaling contradiction. As in Goto's narrative, cultural hybridity is registered through food as a signifying domain. But it is also here another way of ironizing representations of nationhood, of revealing their complicity with ideology, just as it serves to examine the relation of gender to subjectivity. For, if Hannelore renounces Germany as the unhappy past, she clings to it as gastronomic tradition, mysteriously invested with healthy "pure" teutonic value, in the same way that the Falls are invested with sublime mystery. Despite the fact that in the displaced German delicatessen, "the only other Germans available were Bavarian", to her dismay, since she had "so looked forward to speaking German with other Germans", Hannelore is nonetheless drawn to the counter with "metal threads that pulled at [her] eyelids and body like fish hooks" (Mayr 1998, 30). A complex web of thresholds of values and perceptions, of matter and non-matter, here defines the relation between the displaced and those gustatory objects of desire and nostagia. The "[a]ccented Southern German" she "could cut with a knife and spear with a fork and bury in creamed horseradish" (31), means that language and food share the same signifying space of desire and identification; they establish the body here as the central focus of a "reading" of culture itself. That the whole chaotic set-up of a not-really German Bavarian in a not-really Bavarian costume but in a kind of askew German-Canadian combination, presents a heterogeneity of ethnic categorizing and sub-typing, and turns the whole question of category-construction itself into a farce. Moreover, as "both ...

a genre and a preparation in food" (Serres cited in Omhovère 2002c, 131, footnote 22) the concept of farce, as it is deployed here through food, buffoonery, and genre disruption, highlights the transgressive aspects of the narrative. (Claire Omhovère is here referring to Michel Serres' theorizing of the link between satire and farce in their culinary and textual dimensions). For the Cartesian mind/body hierarchy is overturned when Hannelore's exclusionary system of cultural values is mediated through her gustatory sensations. Relying on the domain of the alimentary as the structuring premises of thought and judgement, indiscriminately mixing "sex" and "schmeck", thought, smell, and taste, as in, for example: "Hannelore could smell the sex on Frau Schnadelhuber's mind and she wanted to clap on a gas mask to stop the stench" (Mayr 1998, 147), she collapses value hierarchies. Her appreciation of Hamish as "a mass of [b]izarre male folds and thicknesses" with "strange wandering hairs straggling out of his nose, his ears, the hint of roses among the rotten cabbages" (182), deploys the carnivalesque rhetoric of disruption as a strategy. Such descriptions mix sensory thresholds with those of intelligence and matter, blurring the ontological domains which establish a moral distancing and naturalize values.

Furthermore, the "gray, in-between area of the mixed, the ambiguous" which characterizes much of such description can be linked, via the carnivalesque theme of "the monstrous" to the liminal zone of the originary body, the mother's, one which as "threshold of existence is both sacred and soiled, holy and hellish" (Kristeva cited in Braidotti 1994, 81 – Braidotti is here drawing on Julia Kristeva's theorizing of abjection).

Such "gray areas" of the archaic maternal body seem equally at work in the "wet ribbed inside of a fish" (Mayr 1998, 12) characterizing a throat, or Clotilde's "amphibian tongue" (36), "her head sliced off from the rest of her body" in the swimming-pool, "her eyes round and shiny" (114). Stressing an amorphous, foetal state of semiotic flow and incompletion, the narrative gives us not only "monstrous" images of transformation and inversion but also signals the sacred/soiled dichotomy as a constitutive, though subversive part of feminine/maternal representations in culture. Since: "The fact that [in pregnancy] the female body can change shape so drastically is troublesome in the eyes of the logocentric economy within which to see is the primary act of knowledge and *the gaze* the basis of all epistemic awareness." (Braidotti 1994, 80). Just as the fantasy of ingurgitating and being ingurgitated pertains to femininity and its ambivalent thresholds – since the source of all procreation is the all-powerful "devouring" mother – so it concerns the "devouring" of the mother by the foetus (see Kristeva 1981, chapter 9, where she discusses nature/culture thresholds pertaining to motherhood).

The amorphous images in the narrative where water figures large (wave-pools, the Falls), have something distinctly foetal about them, recalling the illogical "more than one" of maternity itself, a state from which was derived "the special role that the *imagination* plays in the seventeenth century theories of knowledge ... caught in great ambivalence ... [an] ambivalence which we find projected massively onto the power of the mother. She can direct the fetus to normal development or she can de-form it, un-do it, de-humanize it." To such fear and hatred of the feminine in the age of the enlightenment, has been attributed the Cartesian rationale, one which feminists have dubbed: "I think therefore *he* is" (Braidotti 1994, 87).

Braidotti refers again to Kristeva when she states that male anxiety about the representation of feminine difference is linked to "the psychic and cultural imperative to separate from the mother and accept the Law-of-the-Father". For the incest taboo is "built on the mixture of fascination and horror that characterizes the feminine/maternal object of abjection" (1994, 82). Maternity and its attendant cultural anxieties can therefore be seen as contributing to the symbolic erasure, the "Othering" of the female gender in representation.

The rhetorical figuring of excess, of life and death, of blurred limits of inside and outside in *The Widows*, could therefore be seen as the manipulation of conventions of the carnivalesque grotesque in the interests of a feminine problematic of the body, desire and representation. As Hannelore stares at the Falls, "the water rushing and licking over the rim of the cliff, thick on the rocks", she ponders that perhaps "liking Kanada was like having an infection" (Mayr 1998, 21). In its intimate blending of the sublime and the body, the transcendent and the material, this recalls Bhakhtin's analysis of the carnivalesque as "the degradation that is the lowering of all that is high, spiritual, ideal, abstract ... to the material level", to "the life of the belly and the reproductive organs" (Bakhtin 1984, 19-21).

In all these inversions, connections and realignments the narrative clearly links problems of language to both ethnicity and female "Otherness". However, it simultaneously stresses the ultimately performative aspect of culture and subjectivity. For Frau Schnadelhuber's ridiculous Bavarian get-up and Hamish's kilt which define them ethnically through the conventions of visible difference, create categories but at the same time designate ethnicity as costume, challenging notions of ethnic categories themselves. Their real social invisibility,

behind the mask of "ethnic visibility" (which establishes a stereotypical "visible difference" as the only definition of ethnicity), their lack
of influence in a world where the old, female, and marginalized have
no say, represent precisely the grotesque body of "the people" put to
work as recuperative strategy. Dress as costume takes the uniformity
of appearance which stereotypes and marginalizes all those who are
different from the "norm", and plays with the mechanisms of that
containment, turning the "uniforms" inside out as it were. In this context, Frau Schnadelhuber's fake Dirndl Kleid and plaits both identify
her as "ethnic" and identify such "ethnicity" as a vestimentary, artifi-
cially coded sign. When, furthermore, Frau Schnadelhuber sees her
apparent "ethnic" identification as part of the job description, and
when the whole facade implodes into farce in a scene of seduction
with Clotilde, where the Bavarian plaits unwind and the Dirndl gets
man (or rather woman-) handled, reality far exceeds the limits of visibility as a reliable source of knowledge. The buffoonery of the carnivalesque is put to work in transgressing fixed assumptions on
ethnicity just as representation(s) and language are caught up in the
whole play of shifting perceptions on feminine identity.

Falling for the Falls

If playing with costume, with the visible, and the elaboration of
knowledges (and our ways of apprehending the other), is part of a
carnivalesque appropriation, the Niagara Falls also figure as a slippery
signifier, meaning, as we are explicitly told, "everything and nothing",
since they "refuse to be merely a symbol" (Mayr 1998, 229). As
"wondrous" and "monstrous" (20) they exceed all rational capture;
essentially performative they play out whatever is required of them.
As tourist mecca, national icon, litter dump and suicide venue where
"bright flashing lights of the police cruisers and ambulances give their
flamboyant Good Morning" (229), they seem to say nothing more
than their own construction as North American myth and nothing less
than the North American "meaning" of capitalist dream and power
erected as a musical comedy with its combination of bathos and glitz,
as the carnivalesque underbelly of the all-powerful signifier "the
West". As Coral Ann Howells points out in her analysis of the Canadian wilderness as myth, (but what she says seems equally pertinent in
analysing the way natural sites in general are erected as icons): "Wilderness has multiple functions – as geographical location marker, as
spatial metaphor, and as Canada's most popular cultural myth" (Howells 1996, 21). As Culture parading as Nature, a "costumed" actor in

the landscape of hype and masquerade, with its "outrageously sparkling water" (Mayr, 1998, 229), the "real" Falls are part of a strategy
which plays out the theme and textual figure of "Niagara" in the story
as cultural performance.

Several levels of performance are indeed involved here. For, from
the very beginning, which unfolds from the moment of Annie's historical and historicized performance, the narrative explores that "ex-
ploitation in the music halls" (Berton cited in Mayr 1998, 1), which
represents both Annie's disdain for popular entertainment and her
ironic fate as she indeed becomes the focus of the musical rewriting of
her feat. Furthermore, it is *Niagara! the Musical* which fires Hannelore's enthusiasm for the exploit itself, thus putting the performative
at the centre of the plot's motivation. As such the Falls are given multiple shifting perspectives, both as travelling show and tacky artefact.
The lit-up miniature in the theatre lobby both crystalizes and articulates the various strands of repetition and reinvention that make of
Niagara in all its guises a centre of fascination for Hannelore. If *Niagara! the Musical* leads her to the Falls in order to effect her own re-
play of history – the tacky copy thus engendering the act itself – it
also motivates other reinventions. That, for example, of the starlet
from Stettler, Alberta, Ingeborg Kavorkian, who becomes the more
socially acceptable Anglo-Saxon Sharon Lee Silver. That of the whole
foursome of women who steal the ball and rollick across the Canadian
countryside in picaresque fashion, Cleopatra Maria's mechanical pen-
cil making "fastidious ... markings, the multicoloured veins all over
the map indicating twisting roads and rivers" (Mayr 1998, 218-9), in
the fashion of a cartographer/surgeon registering the shifts and con-
vulsions of the land. All roads in the narrative thus inevitably lead to
the Falls and find some sort of accommodation: Cleopatra comes to
terms with the slightly askew family she has instead of the one she
wishes to have, and Hamish's bereavement at the loss of his space-
ball is compensated by the knowledge that it is being used in its allot-
ted role, getting the exposure it deserves instead of gathering dust in
the tunnels of a theatre.

Furthermore, once the women reach their destination Niagara Falls
continue to produce and transform meanings as Annie breaks through
the bounds of mortality and the borders of genre, emerging from the
watery depths of history to encounter "Cleopatra Maria [who] ... no
therapist, ... prepares herself as best she can anyway to deal with a
depressed and furious 158-year-old woman" (237). For Annie lends
her mythic appellation "Queen of the Mist" to the delicatessen, which,
with its fake windows with paintings of "German fields full of yellow

flowers and the Rocky mountains in the distance" (247), provides a suitable venue for the curious family's continuing hybrid existence.

Yet, all the roads leading to an accommodation of difference also trace Canadian symbolic territory as irreduceable to a singular interpretation, as that of multiple thresholds whereby feminine identity and its complicity with, or resistance to, official versions is registered. This challenge to unitary identity and singular versions is posed at the close of *The Widows* in the ironical, and oxymoronic comment on the ever contradictory nature of the everyday. For, as Hannelore states: "The shopping mall is fine, the delicatessen is fine, everything is fine, everything is too fine" (247).

The Female Subject as "Other": Symbolic Locations and Dislocations

Evelyn Lau, *Other Women* and *Runaway: Diary of a Street Kid*: Consumer Culture, Exotic "Other"

The works studied in this section present female identity as a problem explicitly centred within language and the symbolic relation of "Self to "Other" within representation. As such, the focus differs from the historical revisions studied so far. Here I examine the way both Evelyn Lau and Nicole Brossard (albeit in radically different ways, and from opposite sides of the Canadian linguistic border), negotiate the limits of perception and symbolic positioning which structure the subject, and the possible (or impossible) emergence of a feminine difference within representation. Both writers – Lau covertly, Brossard overtly – deal with the problematical envisaging of a subject position from which to speak, and with female subjecthood as a borderline position of shifting affiliations. For Brossard's translation strategies, and Lau's textual grappling with meanings that fall away from any viable discursive positioning, are ways of interrogating symbolic thresholds, of making the interstices register that which the text delivers with difficulty, of finding a way out of the strictures of plot and its constructing of stable meanings.

Asiancy and Agency

A traditional Chinese background, which, as I attempt to demonstrate, is not exempt from its own discursive containments and exclusions, and on the other a North American individualistic, consumerist ethos have moulded Evelyn Lau's subjective positioning. Her work is heavily autobiographical; her past as a teenage drug-addict and prostitute was both the source material of the best-seller *Runaway: Diary of a Street kid* and since has spilled over into the public domain in a media circus about her personal life and relationships, nurtured largely by her own heavily publicized admissions. Since boundaries between her diary, her fiction, and her life tend to blur, she has thus provided a forum for an ongoing debate on the responsibility of the ethnic author towards his/her work. This problematical relationship of author to text, under debate by feminist and postcolonial critics, focusses on agency and "truth" value, on the responsibility of the social, public persona towards his or her literary production, therefore on the intersection of the literal and the literary. This is of course a particularly crucial domain of investigation when it concerns writers whose interest is first and foremost a coming-to-voice, that is, whose writing is at stake in a bid for a recovery of agency wrested from the margins of "official" histories which have, until recently, excluded them. In other words, for some of those writers, as I have attempted to demonstrate through the modes of cultural hybridity already investigated here, "writing the self" is a crucial move in the project for becoming recognized not only in literary terms but in existential ones as well. In this context, the types of self-representations which Lau projects through her work into the public domain, seem to have discredited her in terms of implicit rules of "ethnic correctness": a somewhat ironic turning of the tables of discourses of exclusion when those often relegated to the position of the "Other" in turn relegate to the margins.

As such Jan Wong's article in the *The Globe and Mail* provides an interesting example of the way the dialectic of "Centre" and "Margins" has a way of perpetuating systems of oppositions from which even those with an interest in affranchisement from such systems are not exempt. How "Asiancy" seems to carry an automatic commitment to the furthering of a certain (and apparently exclusive) image of the community as a whole. Wong invokes her own experience of growing up in a Chinese family in Canada as "[t]he kind [of family] who consider friends a frivolity and an 89 per cent exam mark a failure" (1997, C1). Yet, according to Wong: "Millions of Canadians have overcome such traumas, if that is the word, without self-indulgent melt-downs" (C1).

The interesting point here is not whether Lau's work is self-indulgent, but the way that a voice from the "Margins" automatically seems to entail a responsibility to the community, and the way the community in question is represented here by Wong in the same type of "shut-up and put-up" discourse as that of the "Centre" to which it is frequently the "Margins". Lau's work is exemplary in its revealing and problematizing of the discursive nature of identity itself, and the doublebind of community/mainstream affiliations; how Lau has been constructed as "unruly" daughter through the discourse of "proper"

Canadian- Asiancy just as she has been constructed as exotic "Other" within normative discourse. It has to be said that she herself, in her ongoing self-reconstruction through the media, contributes to the confusion between textual and self-representation. As both a mediatized performance and a representative of an erased community voice, Lau is necessarily a vexing and conflictual figure. Moreover, she crystalizes the problem at the heart of any discussion of postcolonial voice and agency, namely that on the one hand any discourse of identity risks congealing into orthodoxy through its appeal to "essential" characteristics, and on the other hand, the risk of possible failure of insertion into a viable historical narrative through the reduction of identity to the mere free play of signifiers. This double bind in the structuring of identity itself, which, it seems to me, is foregrounded in the "production" of Lau as literary persona, is underlined by Slavoj Žižek when he claims that "ideology ... consolidates itself not through expected conformity to its imperatives but rather through regulated transgression" (cited in Beauregard 1999, 58). Lau's "life-writing" in its disorderly dimension thus aggravates the existing tension around the sites of struggle for emergence of Asian-Canadian literature. It also brings to the fore the debates within feminist theory and the struggle for change since similar, often confrontational, perspectives on political/social action versus women's symbolic, discursive inscription within representation are apparent.

When speaking on the ambivalent relationship of Lau to her public image, the critic Smaro Kamboureli has suggested that she buys into the enlightenment paradigm disseminated in Canadian national pedagogies which promote a "post-ethnicity", a "we have arrived" idea of progress, embracing a recuperative multicultural policy which, instead of promoting difference, seeks to contain it. (Kamboureli was speaking at the Marburg Canadian Literature Day, June 13, 2001).

Yet whilst Kamboureli's argument is cogent it may not be the whole story as far as Lau is concerned. Since, in a way and once again, it crystalizes the whole problem of writing and responsability which Lau continually raises, whilst implying that at no level can Lau's "post-ethnic", uncritical writing escape its own (apparently) capitalistic, assimilationist ideals. I would maintain, rather, that Lau's diary and fiction provide a fraught encounter between various types of institutional discourses and their limits, which reveals the ideological underpinnings of *all* discursive positions. It is indeed true that her fictional representations are predicated in the stereotypical grammars of exoticism and pornography, belonging to a sex-industry which contributes to consolidating the image of the Chinese woman as a glamorous object. Yet the conflicted encounter between both codified and more shifting identifications in her work, the way the limits of stereotypical formulas are foregrounded, and the way subject positions are both established and problematized, reveal the complex workings of subjectivity within Western liberalism where hybrid cultural identity is not comfortably contained. As Sneja Gunew points out: "women and migrants internalize the process whereby the culture constructs them, and it requires a great deal of self-conscious analysis before they are able to step (and only ever in part) outside these constructs" (Gunew 1995, 124).

It is the purpose here to demonstrate how Lau's work effectively both underlines and challenges the meshing of mainstream cultural discourses and the voice of the subject, showing that binary oppositions are not only at work in the elaboration of an imperial "Centre" to its excluded "Others" but that they are what makes any (Western) cultural discourse possible, to the extent that defining one's identity is necessarily a positional act, one of exclusion as much as inclusion. Lau is therefore both within and outside versions of identity, which does not preclude discursive thresholds and overlappings. What enables "difference", at the same moment that it disavows it, is precisely the textual negotiation in Lau's work, the blurring of limits at the critical juncture of a coming-to-voice as an act of affirmation, and the available social, cultural, intimate grammars in which such a coming-to-voice of a Chinese-Canadian ex-junky, ex-prostitute could be coherently encoded.

Runaway: or Whose Self Is It Anyway?

The diary, which attracted much media attention, is a thematic introduction to her fiction since, although it is a factual account of Lau's running away from home and her years on the streets riding the merry-go-round of drugs and prostitution, similar power relations of older men and young girls are equally at work in her fiction. While the diary has mainly been acclaimed on the strength of its insights into the street *milieu*, the object here is not to dwell on the misery and degradation which are undoubtedly its themes. I prefer to look at the ways in which the journal reads as a "trying on of selves" in the sense of the various socio/psycho/medical discourses through which the transgressive Lau is "restructured", and which are themselves the sign of a liberal, capitalistic (thus reproductive) ideology at work.

Michel Foucault has discussed the relation between the personal experience of selfhood and the social/political terms of such experience. He moves from the question 'what is the Self?' to 'on what grounds is my identity based?'" (Foucault 1994, 791, translation mine) Lau's diary, entirely caught up in investigating a self in distress is not only an individual's bid to "find herself" but could be seen as an interrogation of the discursive grounds on which such a coherent identity could be founded.

As such, the form of Lau's account diverges from traditional Western autobiographical writing, writing which engages in "generalizing the particular, fabricating a narrative space of familiarity, and crafting a narrative that links the individual to the universal" (Kaplan 1998, 212). As an "outlaw" genre the journal makes no attempt to create a linear narrative of progression of the individual, but (rather exhaustingly at times), presents the radical swings of pessimism and optimism of Lau's attempts to come to terms with her family background, and to break the spiral of dependency on drugs (and, one is tempted to say, on the social/psychological purveyors of discourses on "self-management"). The journal continually passes from a discourse of liberal progressive optimism of "get a job, get a flat, get a coherent self", to the pull of the night world where such dictates seemingly break down. Yet one can in fact wonder whether the reader's exhaustion is not due to the fact that the "Margins" of society explored by Lau are merely the "Other" side of the logic of consumer capitalism functioning along the same lines; a logic whereby the same market place economics and range of illusions, disillusions, idealisms and satisfactions are played out through the succession of "customers" Lau presents us with. Within this dialectic of inside and outside as mutually dependent cultural spaces, the tragedy for the self-searching teenager resides in the discovery that forays into the world of drugs and prostitution do nothing to enable a transgression of codes. Rather, her exploration of a world unknown to most readers reveals that there is no transcending of such codes themselves, at least in the way the Western world is moving; that our liberal model of individualism is itself founded on a fundamental subject/object dichotomy. Looked at from this angle one could see the journal as revealing more about the institutional forces at work (and I include the "sex industry" as one such institution), than the "self" which Lau does or does not "find". It becomes an engagement with the available discourses of truth and identity and the way "self-invention, self-discovery, and self-representation emerge within the technologies of autobiography – namely, those legalistic, literary, social, and ecclesiastical discourses ... through which the subject is produced" (Gilmore 1998, 184).

Thus, it seems to me that *Runaway* incites an interpretation of the kind which Leigh Gilmore calls "[a]utobiographics, as a description of self-representation and as a reading practice" (184). For whereas the journal thematizes the teenager's desire for adequate self-representation in the world(s) she inhabits, this desire puts her at the centre of a mass of legal, social and psychiatric interests and discourses. She is pushed from one jurisdiction to the another, between care workers and the police, children's homes and psychiatrists. She indeed becomes, an "object of knowledge", materialized as subject according to a number of contracts of socialization which are themselves "defined, invested with value, recommended, imposed" (Foucault 1994, 213, translation mine). Her status as a social outsider puts her in direct contact with a multiplicity of institutional discourses which all make concerted efforts to transform a disturbed teenager into a model citizen.

Runaway is in some ways reminiscent of Ken Loach's film *Family Life*, in which an imaginative teenager of a repressed English household in the cultural revolution of the 1960s, is submitted to a variety of psychiatric discourses and practices through which the limits of institutional adjustment to a radically changing social climate are foregrounded. For lack of an available social discourse within which the girl could express herself, in an England caught between a creaking Victorian morale and emancipation, she becomes the object of, and is sacrificed to, medical science's investigation into its own limits.

The overwhelming pressure of medical science in *Runaway*, in an age which prefers remedial therapy to an in-depth questioning of social and institutional policy, presents a similar foregrounding of limits, pitted against Lau's desire to "speak" herself. The constant intervention of psychiatry in the diary testifies to its influence on and interaction with the various "self-representations" which Lau presents to the reader; Lau as scientific object becomes increasingly entangled with the status of a subject-in-the-making which the diary form generally expresses. After having idealized the social worker she later denigrates his "stilted, rehearsed voice" (Lau 1989, 52), and yet unquestioningly takes on board the recommendations of the psychiatrist and his multiple interpretations of her state: "Come on Evelyn! You can do better than spend the rest of your life standing around downtown ... So what do you want to be, A teenybopper? A *preppy*? ... Okay, so we were wrong were we? You don't want to be anything better than the thousands of others!" (118). Which is not to say, I hasten to add, that individuals in the medical sciences or any other science are ill-intentioned, or that it was not in Lau's personal interest to seek help to stop her self-destructive cycle. The interest here lies in the way her diary intensely registers and is pressured by the self/other dialectic which affects (infects?) the structuring of the codes and practices of civil and personal life.

It is equally interesting to note that the problem not addressed by the authorities which treat her is perhaps at least one of the most pertinent to an analysis of her state, namely, her status as Asian-Canadian. As the daughter of a traditional Chinese family expecting obedience and continuous study, in conflict with the teenage world around her, Lau is from the outset caught up in a complex array of often conflictual expectations, which do not only stem from her fraught relations with over-zealous parents, but also with the way they themselves relate to/are integrated in Canada, and the terms of that integration. That they should drive to see their daughter succeed in the Canadian "New World" liberal economy is understandable, but that Evelyn's adopted role as "bright, industrious Chinese" at school should merely enhance a stereotyping, (which is articulated in another way when she becomes the exotic Asian prostitute), reveals the source of her problem with "belonging" which haunts the account. When faced with her parents' checking up on her attendance at school Lau is "ENRAGED", feeling she could "NEVER BE FREE OF THEM IN VANCOUVER" (86). Yet, just as life at home was, in Lau's words, one swallowing endless hell" (266), life with her schoolmates was equally a bid for "acceptance" which she wanted "as desperately as anyone else" (272). That her therapist addresses her torment of living at home but does not, or cannot, either place it in the context of her parents integration and its price, or within the context of the cultural rift opened up within Lau herself in her belonging to two worlds, reveals the blind spot in his own vision. In fact Lau's integration, her "cure", will dismiss the real historical "inbetweenness" of her status, and the therapy only seek to recuperate her via the Freudian paradigm of the Oedipal relationship, whereby parent/child conflicts are resolved through the apprenticeship of separation and "becoming your own person". But, one is tempted to ask, from what premises of relinquishment is Lau's "own person" to emerge, and from what cultural erasure is becoming an "Asian-Canadian" in fact more about becoming "Asian on Canadian terms?" As the critic Arnold Itwaru has theorized, foregrounding clearly the problem of self-image and self-representation as a complex dialectic in the act of migration:

...the wish to cross over, the alleged magical transformation realizable only in the thereness of the other, necessitates the subject's conception of selfhood on the basis of outsidership. Self seen in terms of the negating other is self-negation. The

negating of self-negation intensifies the image of the other as the embodiment of
desire. ... Thus is created the subject as non-being (Itwaru 1990, 87-8).

Itwaru goes on to attribute this debilitating cycle of unequality to a
positivism through which the West, and in this case Canada, is invented as "an especially powerful souce of attraction" and is promoted
as an ideal world where "notions of progress, prosperity, and educa-
tional development are made manifest"(88).

That in her diary Lau's therapy does not historically contextualize
the "hell" of home within the larger problems of the family's integra-
tion/outsidership serves to shed light on the discursive limits governing the teenager's see-saw of transgression and rehabilitation. It also
goes some way towards explaining the self-consciousness and "closed
circuit" effect that transpires from the writing itself. In the context of
Smaro Kamboureli's theorizing on Canada's multiculturalist "sedative
politics", and the fact that "when the ethnic subject speaks of and
through herself, she does so by interpreting how she has already been
constructed" (Kamboureli 2000, 1994), Lau's writing does seem contained by the structuring limits of a Canadian policy producing "suitable" ethnic subjects for liberal discursive management. But
discourses precisely have edges and limits, ones which are particularly
mobile and critical when history, family tradition, immigration and
liberalism meet within the all too easily exoticized Asian female subject. It is at the edges of the Law-of-the-Father governing the so-
cio/symbolic that such crucial, textual indices are signalled, there
where contradictory subjective identifications both partake in, and
exceed discursive management.

However, the question indeed remains whether Lau, in her mediatized "performative" life, and in her writing, does not ultimately
reveal the limits and internal contradictions of Canadian, liberal pedagogies aiming at embracing cultural difference but which inevitably
recuperate that difference as managed "Other" within Western, mainstream ideologies. The dominant feature of all kinds of imperialisms,
has long been a faculty to reproduce the "Centre" on the territory of
the prohibited (thus sexually fantasized) exotic female "Other". The
reading of her novel *Other Women* which follows will focus on the
way the female subject is both an overdetermined object of Western
representations and also goes some way to exceeding those encodings.

Other Women: Who Speaks for Whom and from Where?

Other Women, which relates the obsession of a young artist for a
married business man, bears all the hallmarks of the stereotypical

romance plot; "Sunset Beach" revisiting the Freudian drama of how to wrest Daddy from the arms of a hopelessly more deserving (since legitimate) woman. The narrative presents a succession of "takes" on the subject: the narrator Fiona in a hotel with the mysterious lover, in the gym, in shops, in California. Surfaces seem to stand in for setting, themselves part of a decor where emotion is inseparable from cliché, the latter lending a frozen, formulaic quality to the former. Nostalgia permeates such phrases as "Two weeks before the end of our affair, I had come to California to stand on a famous street corner and think of you" or "I walked the length of the dying boulevard whispering your name, but you did not come" (Lau 1995, 49). Everything in the narrative seems to fall back into a discursive containment, a kind of "primal scene" scenario of exclusion, endlessly revisited in different configurations, as it relates the narrator's forays into the anonymous world of bars, hotels and clubs, into interchangeable spaces characterized by the reproductive values of hi-tech capitalism.

Yet, the narrative goes some way to subverting its own strategies of framing; one such area of play is the economy of sight in which the symbolic pact of self-reflection which stabilizes presence, is here both textually worked and interrupted. Self-reflective moments abound in the narrative: when the narrator Fiona "sees herself in the mirror ... her body emerging inside the antique frame" or her lover is "gazing through the peephole", or when he "looks at her with the direct, disinterested gaze of a stranger" (1-2), to cite but a few examples of many. Subjective presence is here deferred as connections between looking subject and object of the gaze fail.

As Peggy Phelan has observed in *Unmarked: The Politics of Performance*, the gaze and the returned gaze of the other are fundamental structuring elements in self-representation: "The eyes look out; one needs always the eye of the other to recognize (and name) oneself. In other words the gaze guarantees the *failure* of self-seeing" (Phelan 1993, 15). Lau's symbolic breaking points thus crystalize the ambivalence of self-representation in that they repeatedly signal the fundamental contradiction of subjecthood: that symbolic castration is the necessary prerequisite for subjective integration, precisely because the contradictory truth "[a]ll seeing is hooded with loss" (16) is the prerequisite of all symbolic exchange.

The multiple specular images whereby Fiona seeks to confirm her presence in fact disarticulate a coherent focus and present instead fractured perceptions. For when she seeks her image in the gym, it is "to lose [herself]" (Lau 1995, 56), and as she "turn[s] in a store's mirror, wearing a new skirt", she sees neither herself nor the fantasized lover she hopes to see but "Jessica asking for assistance" (60).

We can look to Phelan again when she says that sight is eminently discursive as: "The positions which define the distinction between the subject and the object in the visual field are psycho-linguistic" (Phelan 1993, 15). In *Other Women* therefore, these congealed moments of structuring/disconnection signal what is at stake in the emergence of the female speaking subject as a discursive, symbolic positioning. They also problematize, by their simultaneous focus on narcissistic confirmations of self-identity and by the narrator's erasure from these reflections, the meaning of representation itself as far as women are concerned, and in particular those women who are easily marginalized or exoticized, situated somewhere between objective and subjective positionings.

Other symbolic disjunctions in the narrative are taken up by Sneja Gunew as the counter-point to the "excesses of sexual perversion and addiction [which] serve to confirm social standards since the norm or measure is always present as a point of nostalgic invocation" (Gunew 1998, 259). For, as Gunew rightly says, and in a similar fashion to *Runaway*, *Other Women* is about "the reconfirmation of the yuppie heterosexual couple as a constitutive norm for sexual-social relations" (259). However, as she goes on to affirm, the disjunctions between body and voice in the narrative, and the importance of sound over sight in the narrator's identifications serve to exceed the stereotypical themes. We can in any case surmise, that whether one focusses on the problematising of subjective emergence and positioning in the realm of sight, or sees the narrator as a disembodied subject of speech in the domain of sound, what transpires from *Other Women* is that the codes which reiterate the desirable social norm in the novel are also the means of their subversion. Such symbolic displacements, resulting in constantly shifting narrative frames, actually challenge those stable subject positionings and points of reference which the nostalgia and cliché work to establish. The narrator's triangular relationship, her fantasized identifications with both the lover and his wife, set up a play of narrative displacements through which the narrator is figured both as subject and object. As Fiona listens to her lover on the phone to his wife, her positioning in the scene shifts from subject – "please, just turn round and look at me" – to excluded bystander – "He does not look at the woman on the couch" – or to a fantasized identification with his wife's position – "If Helen were in the room, she would understand; she would see the shape of her husband's body ... keeping it safe from the woman who sits a short distance away" (Lau 1995, 7).

This mobile narratorial positioning also invests the text with a different type of nostalgia: that for a unity, for dyadic symbiosis with the archaic mother of the pre-symbolic realm. It is this working of desire and difference which disrupts the Law-of-the-Father and interrupts the closure apparent in the conventional theme of the love triangle.

I would suggest further that this other scene, or "Other" (unconscious) scene of lack and uncloseability can be related to Homi Bhabha's definition of the postcolonial decentred subject "signified in the nervous temporality of the transitional, or the emergent provisionality of the 'present'" (1994, 216). For *Other Women* is articulated through such "in-between spaces of double frames" where the narrator is caught up in simulacre and surfaces, where shifts in focus signal unstable subjective positionings. Moreover, in the anxious mode of the star-crossed lovers plot, situations and characters do not fit together in the narrative; they fail to meet as they should. The lover is never where he is expected to be, yet he is registered everywhere through the narrator's focus, for whom: "all men contained something that reminded me of you" (Lau 1995, 17).

Such a play of subjective perceptions, of fluid boundaries of the self, is also registered in other types of thresholds: the problematizing of inside and outside where limits register the anxiety of passage, or of crossing over as a problem of representation itself. For cultural anxiety is signalled through displacement, in a passage where the narrator comes back into Canada after a trip to the United States, where she witnesses the customs pulling a writer's manuscript apart, and where she fears for her own safe passage: "Fiona felt surprised and lucky that she had made it so easily across the border. Then she remembered that she was returning to the country of her birth and that she had nothing to declare"(42).

The passage is striking in that the writer stopped by the customs – the Law in the area of national boundaries and protection – points us to Lau herself as a ghostly, writerly presence. For as the narrator fantasizes her own failure of entry into her country she misrecognizes her own national identification and thus, in a moment of self-blindness, erases her origins before remembering what, in a suppression of the very notion of absence itself she had forgotten: that she "had nothing to declare". It is as though the very referential terms on which absence can be registered – its opposition to presence – has here been suppressed, leaving us with an ontological gap, a lack of any stable point of reference in the form of a trace, which could anchor the narrator in a place called "home".

This anxiety and repression could be analysed as a textual symptom of Lau's place on the border space (See Wong 2001, 129) as Chinese-Canadian, her writing an anxiety of authorship in the domain of the social, cultural Symbolic, the phallocentric Law of propriety and "Proper" Canadian identity. Such moments, when the shadow of Lau as textual effect ghosts the narrative and problematizes the notion of origins signal the working-over of desire, which "speaks ... in the un-sutured gaps of discourse, disrupting, displacing, seeking satisfaction or expression, but also offering the possibility of other positions for the subject and confirming the nature of subjectivity as an effect of language" (Cameron 1987, 143).

If, therefore, Lau cannot be comfortably placed in a coherent "reci-tation of the *ethnos*" (Loriggio 1987, 61) which characterizes such Chinese-Canadian writings as Sky Lee's *Disappearing Moon Cafe*, a novel which seeks to retrieve a heritage from the vestiges of cultural erasure, the problem of "who speaks" and "from which position" is nonetheless raised in Lau's fiction. Her non-adherence to a legible script of ethnicity, for which she has been taken to task, does not therefore mean that "*ethnos*" is absent from her writing. It emerges precisely in the difficulty of locating a coherent site from which to speak, within the tensions of positioning, in the encounter with the Law of the cultural, social hegemony.

If, therefore, *Other Women*'s pre-occupation with the body as sex-ual instrument and with the eroticism of illicit liaisons is an aspect of the novel's containment in discourses of heteronormativity which contribute to the impression of "dirty realism", and to the impression of not only celebrating the rise of the penis but that of the phallus as transcendent signifier, we can perhaps look beyond the closure of Lau's themes to the disruptive textual strategies which are precisely the "Other" side of such clichéd representations.

That the writer herself further disrupts the distinctions between body and text, between "mind-work" and "body-work" in her own disturbing "recitations of identity", can explain the quandary into which she throws critical appraisals. But perhaps Lau's interest lies precisely in the pressure she puts on our Western, academic, critical distinctions between discursive domains, distinctions which we, rather uncomfortably, have interest in wishing to collapse as well as to pre-serve intact.

Nicole Brossard, *Mauve Desert*: Crossings and Sitings

The spiral pattern opens out onto the unwritten. And the unwritten circulates, round and round, producing emanations like those at the door to an initiatory pathway (Brossard 1989, 14).

The Quebec separatist movements of the 1970s and a concomitant feminist awareness put Nicole Brossard at the forefront of writings which sought to challenge the phallogocentric roots of culture and language itself. Much like van Herk, Brossard's writing is character- ized by a political and theoretical drive; the former's "geografictione" and "crypto-frictions" are matched by the latter's "fiction-theory", elaborated in *The Aerial Letter*. The twelve texts of this study consti- tute a theoretical journey into "the signifying process of language to reveal its arbitrary and biased nature and to transgress its conventions" (Brossard 1988, 20). The metaphors which Brossard has elaborated from the 70s on – for example the "spiral" and the "hologram" – are critical levers applied to both cultural and fictional representations. Like Hélène Cixous or Luce Irigaray, Brossard sees the social/cultural aspect of feminine gender representations as deriving from the non- emergence of a female subject position within language itself. Her work thus focusses on those edges of representation where a feminine "sense [can be] *renewed*, through excursions into and explorations of non-sense", thus offering "new configurations of woman-as-being-in- the-world" (117). Since such transformations rely on an economy of desire, such an apprehension of women's bodies as the site of a "text matter" (68), of a signifying difference, has invited a reading of Brossard's feminist politics as essentialist. Yet such a reading seems to ignore the philosophical thrust of such theory; confusing the body as the material site of subjecthood, both informing and informed by social, symbolic and political knowledges, with a biological deter- minism. Brossard is not concerned with remaking and "re-marking" "Woman" as the negative pole in a nature/culture binary, but rather with her possible emergence as female speaking subject, with women's access to meaning. Such a critical/fictional process entails investigating not the body *per se*, but the bodily roots of female sub- jectivity as sexually differentiated, where alterity provides an enabling dynamics since it strives precisely to undo women's overdetermina- tion within the nature/culture scenario.

I would therefore agree with Winfried Siemerling that in Brossard's work "the space of incomplete knowledge appears ... as the mobile figure of an other both inside and outside, ... an unknown as an ena- bling form of alterity that it produces, and by which it is produced"

(Siemerling 1994, 183). Her work has tended, within a specifically Quebecois and feminist context, towards interrogating the material roots of subjectivity and the way language – in particular in realistic fiction – naturalizes the abstracted, homogeneous forms it in fact produces. Breaking the coherence of such forms is therefore a political move, a challenging of both fictional and political closures through the textual inscription of a sexualized, thus differentiated, female subjectivity in language. Furthermore, as Sherry Simon points out, language has always played a fundamental role in defining cultural difference in Canada since "for more than two centuries the political, economic and cultural life of Canada has been accounted for in terms of its 'founding peoples' ... [whereby] language has been persistently maintained as the essential sign of difference between the two groups" (1992, 159).

If Brossard's work has been closely linked to the political upheavals and Quebec separatist movements of the 70s, she has since then, like other feminists, challenged the nationalist movement's intentions. For if "for many early female separatists, the nationalist movement ... seemed to be a forum through which women could challenge their double marginalisation as Québécoise (*sic*)" the equating of Quebec as "the mother, as *terre Québec*" (Verwaayen 1977, 2) in texts of the 60s reveals the phallocentricity which ultimately dismissed feminist interests in the name of the nationalist cause.

Brossard has also gone further than a passive identification with oppressed womanhood in general, regarding the task of writing as "a matter of life and death", carrying the responsibility of elaborating "new meaning" (Brossard 1993, 65). As such, Brossard's "fiction-theory" is a politics within which "lesbian" does not so much characterize a social positioning and a sexual preference as a radical discursive strategy, one which stems from the way the space occupied by lesbianism "in a patriarchal, heterosexual world", made "life absolute fiction" (60) for Brossard herself. It is from this positioning both inside and outside existing discursive modalities in the heterosexual world that Brossard's investigations emanate, from her experience both of life as a mother and as a lesbian. Such a subjective positioning within and astride multiple socio/symbolic spaces affords her an accrued perception of the boundaries policing such spaces, and of the conflictual workings of ideology within mainstream culture. It is a similar conception of cultural limits and the invention of forms which we find at work in her novel *Mauve Desert*.

Deleuze and Guattari's work on Kafka's writing as "deterritorialized" could provide a model for the kind of textual displacement operated by Brossard. Kafka was a Czech Jew, writing in German, the dominant (bureaucratic) language, and his writing was therefore representative of "a minority writing in a majority language" (Deleuze and Guattari 1975, 29, translation mine), an "impossible" task since neither writing in German nor writing otherwise was an authentic option. If Brossard is culturally a long way from Kafka's Prague, the notion of being both linguistically inside and yet marginalized from the dominant "Centre" of the culture, (and within a Francophone culture itself marginalized within the Anglo-Canadian one), results in a similar process of "deterritorialisation", de-centering the premises on which holistic cultural narratives are constructed. Brossard thus cuts across several critical boundaries: that of Quebec as a francophone "Centre" and yet a Canadian minority in terms of power and influence, that of lesbian, mother and committed feminist; she also makes of language a critical, territorial enterprise.

In *Mauve Desert* the symbolic order is put to the test through strategies which fracture continuity and disrupt stable identifications. Similarly the textual defamiliarisation such alterity produces invents new sets of figures and new cognitive spaces through which novel connections provide the basis for interpretation. Finally, the female body as a source of differential meaning, as both a textual signifier and a sexual signifier of desire, produces the politicized metaphor of the lesbian text, a construct which, according to Brossard, "any woman can claim for herself [since] [t]he lesbian is a mental energy which gives breath and meaning to the most positive of images a woman can have of herself" (Brossard 1985, 121). The lesbian praxis at work here is thus far from an effort to circumscribe writing within the confines of ideological claims or specific group interests, however valid such claims may be. The politically motivated but non-restrictive "lesbian" body that emerges here is at the interface of culture and language, "offering sexual, textual interlinings of surfaces, contours, flow, energies, mechanics" (Holbrook 1997, 233). Ceasing to be the vehicle of "Meaning" it becomes the instrument of meanings.

Translation: a Challenge to Originality

The novel *Mauve Desert* is composed of two "books". Furthermore, it is divided into sections which cut across the kind of logical continuity expected of an autobiographical account. Since the desert of Arizona, where the characters gravitate in and around a motel, is no sooner established as the focus, than the first-person voice is inter-

rupted and the perspective changes to accommodate the enigmatic
presence of Longman, an avatar of the scientist Oppenheimer in the
narrative. Yet just as sections confuse our expectations of continuity,
Mauve Desert equally promises a symmetry which is deferred. For the
novel within the novel seems to offer a copy, just as Laure Angstelle,
writer, and Maude Laures, translator, provide a kind of double. The
"translation" that emerges is part of the fractured mirroring that both
creates identifications and defers them. Instead it opens a "perspective
of the two-way passage" (Brossard 1990, 57), playing both on the idea
of an original and a copy, and establishing a vector of exchange at the
core of the narrative. In its incessant reflections and deflections
Brossard's "intention to *carry over*" (57) refers us to the hologram's
image-production. Since, in much the same way that Brossard con-
ceives fiction as dealing with "'real' characters through imagination"
– the "virtual part of the real" – the hologram "deals with a 'real' object which through 'virtual' image produces a 'fictive' image"
(Brossard 1993, 72). Concerned with the fusion and confusion of levels of reality then, and with the conditions of stable origins, *Mauve
Desert* is a meditation on both textual identity and female subjectivity.

As Karen Gould states, the very ontology of the novel is subjected
to, and destablized through "the themes, emotions, situations and textual strategies already explored in other Brossardian works" (1992,
198, translation mine). Thus, *Mauve Desert* is not only concerned with
the play of identity and difference as a textual aesthetics but inscribes
it within Brossard's continuing engagement with finding ways to "un-
erase", and deliver the feminine signifier from the logic of the
"Same". That this enquiry into forms of knowledge constitutes
Brossard's own "translation" process as she re-evaluates her own "angle of vision" (22, footnote 4) from work to work, situates the textual
strategies of the novel within a project of actively dismantling the
hierarchy between imaginary and "real" social representations; (Karen
Gould has pointed out the frequent use of, and play on, the signifier
"angle" in the novel). She thus implicitly questions the premises on
which "reality" founds its universal value. As Brossard says: "I am
usually writing about acts of passage" (Brossard 1993, 70), and such
crossings between different epistemological domains are intended, as
in *Mauve Desert*, to open up a "new horizon" (72) of meaning. As
such, the blurring of semantic, conceptual and imaginary boundaries
in the novel is characteristic of Brossard's theoretical and fictional
production, in particular when the "book" "Mauve Desert" becomes,
in a "translation" which is not really one, "Mauve the Horizon". A
perspective on women's absence from self-representation is given to

us through the prevalent theme of violence in the narrative, and the subverted genre of the detective story. The unresolved murder of the character Angela Parkins serves both to imaginatively interrogate women's erasure from patriarchal meaning, and to question the history of violence to women. It is a murder which places the novel within a Quebecois literary history which "reproduces all the murders of women which have littered Quebecois texts since the nineteenth century" (Smart 1988, 335).

Furthermore the establishing and then blurring of limits between "translation" and "copy" that the textual strategies develop, lead to a challenging of the premises underlying identity itself. As Susan Holbrook states, the ethos underpinning the translation process combines the concept of source and faithful copy in a fixed relation "of agency, of subordination" whereby "the translator's target text [is] expected to remain ever faithful to the genius of origin" (1997, 234). Embedded within this logic are the more general implications of the hierarchy between "productive and reproductive work" and the "cultural anxieties about paternity [as 'origin', and] women's creativity" (234). Brossard stages this logic within the narrative and subverts it; the "translation" of "Mauve Desert" is neither faithful nor unfaithful: it gestures towards the one-way passage of self-representation which translation exemplifies, but, since there is no "original" at stake, but the performing of one, and thus no "copy", and since both "original" and "copy" co-exist within the same textual dynamics and ontological space, translation becomes truly a question of carrying across, of substituting interaction for domination. Thus the "transformances" of which Holbrook speaks, "celebrating the impossibility of equivalence" (232), which emphasize process, mobility and provisonality rather than product, is an apt description of the forces at work in *Mauve Desert*; (Holbrook is here referring to a translation project between Nicole Brossard and Daphne Marlatt). By displacing the stable "Centre" established within normative translation, the implicitly gendered code of translation is undermined. One which relies on "the concept of fidelity ... used to regulate sex and/in the family, to guarantee that the child is the production of the father, reproduced by the mother" (Chamberlain 1992, 66). The issues of "faithfulness" which govern the translation enterprise and establish an overregulated hierarchy between original and copy are, according to Lori Chamberlain, a sign of that cultural anxiety over origins, a sign of the threat within power structures that reproductions could "masquerade as originals" (67).

Rather than reproducing such a gendered hierarchy, the mode of "carrying over" in the novel, as a textual *corps à corps* between "original" and "copy", seeks out those thresholds of alterity where desire emerges. The translation "sexualizes" the text, not as a substitution, but as a dialogue of the senses through which the subjective points of contact establish signifying differences; it undoes the "property and proprietry" of legitimate paternal origins of meaning in favour of an "unfaithful" mobile form. As such, the narrative offers a logic whereby transcendent "Meaning" is not confirmed and stabilized through its other text as "Other", but one through which the narrative centre of gravity is dispersed. As such the textual play on "angles" on reality, the linking of the two feminine presences Maude and Laure as echoes of a lost symmetry, the almost-repetitions that abound, all serve to re-enact that moment when a stable presence can be identified. Such a moment registers the "two" of translation about to be subsumed in the "unique" and then oscillates between spaces. This threshold, or instance of immediacy, is, to cite Siemerling, "a return to the same ... [a] point of origin that has become other" (Siemerling 1994, 188).

The erosive potential of the textual strategies in *Mauve Desert* recalls what Brossard says on lesbianism in relation to meaning: "Any lesbian is unbearable because she deceives, offends, or invalidates patriarchal sense. ... A lesbian who does not reinvent the Word is a lesbian in the process of disappearing" (Brossard 1988, 122). The bodily confrontation and mutual embracing of the "same-but-other" which the narrative effects, is therefore a philosophical and political move in the name of a critical praxis dismantling the philosophical, gendered, roots of representation.

To this end translation in the narrative represents a continuous process of negotiation between sites of being. When speaking of Brossard and Daphne Marlatt's translation project, Holbrook makes the distinction between a "fluid" as opposed to a "fluent" passage from one language to the other, thus aptly pinpointing the political drive behind Brossard's aesthetic choice of writing mode: fluency in translation is designed to seamlessly effect the return to an "original" text, whereas fluidity blurs distinctions between distinct ontologies. The "lost in translation" which qualifies a normative perspective through which, ideally, the other text is entirely recuperated as a unified, originary presence, becomes in the novel a play of multiple perspectives. Furthermore, the refusal of a hierarchy between source and copy which the translation strategies of the narrative promote, making of both a creative component of the whole, gestures towards the multiple linguistic/discursive spaces that compose the social and political field of culture in general. The hybridity at work in *Mauve Desert* offers a textual structuring of feminine difference, but also posits the Canadian body politic in its hierarchical and conflictual dimensions and points to a Quebecois linguistic and political positioning that is both antagonistic and dualistic, both inside and outside. One could venture the proposition that Brossard's deconstructing of hierarchies and staging of the phallocentric bias of representation equally plays with those national borders which define dominant and dominated within a universalizing, Anglo-Saxon rhetoric. Smaro Kamboureli has dwelt on the "dialectical and diacritical" (2000, 95) rendering of the Canadian Multicultural Act in its French/English versions. She demonstrates the ambivalence of the relationship between the two political entities and the problematizing of concepts of "origin" in relation to Canadian culture that the Act stages. If "a fundamental element in translation, [is] ... the original's 'great longing for linguistic complementation'" (Walter Benjamen cited in Kamboureli 2000, 96), this implies that "translation is primarily a process of *putting* together ... [for it] demonstrates that the 'original', too, is something that has been put together" (Chow cited in Kamboureli 2000, 96). The whole debate on how the foreign "Other" is necessary to the maintaining of the "Centre" as self-presence thus pertains, crucially, to Canada's both dualistic and multi-ethnic reality. The translation process at work in *Mauve Desert* can then be seen as crystalizing the ambivalent and conflictual workings of the diverse inclusions, exclusions and borders which structure both Canadian political and symbolic territories.

When Two Texts Speak Together

The text as a space of alterity and desire recalls Luce Irigaray's theorization of female sexuality and subjecthood in her seminal essay exploring women's relation to pleasure. In "This Sex Which is not One" Irigaray explores women's eroticism which is not reducible to a phallic "one", since "her sexuality always at least double, is in fact *plural*" (Irigaray 1981, 102). Irigaray posits the importance of touch over sight, of contiguity over transcendence in a female economy of desire, one where "[w]oman ... would be protected from dispersion because the other is a part of her, and is autoerotically familiar to her" (104). Irigaray is here not pleading for a biological determinism, but examining the workings of the sexual economy which underpins language, and is looking for ways around the phallogocentric logic of self-identity. The alternative version of multiplicity and plurality

which Irigaray profers as the expression of a repressed female imaginary thus finds a textual corollary in *Mauve Desert*. The semantic
slippages and linguistic slips of the tongue as Brossard plays with
words and concepts – Melanie/"mais-la-nuit" (but the night), who
drives a car called a Meteor; Maude Laures/"mots de Laure" (Laure's
words) – combine matter, night, light within a sensual and textu(r)al
logic (See Patterson 1993, 109-23, translation mine). This logic operates through a series of permutations and figures intricately linking
female desire to language. As Janet Patterson states: "it's a novel,
strange language transgressing logical, discursive limits; a language in
which the sound of consonants and the articulating of the body can be
heard" (118). Thus Brossard seeks to "sexualize" the text and "textu-
alize" the subject; the play of moving between two distinct ontologies,
of "taking on the book body to body", becomes a merging of one in
the other as Maude Laures "slip[s] anonymous and whole between the
pages" (Brossard 1990, 161).

An Anti-*His*tory

As such Brossard creates what Gail Scott has termed a "shadow-
less" writing, a renunciation of the mechanisms of plot, characteriza-
tion and continuity which lend realism its status as a coherent,
apparently independent world (see Scott 1989). The group of women
in the desert – a kind of zero point of civilisation – gives onto both
violence (in the shape of Longman/Oppenheimer) and horizons which
are presaged beyond the codes of the symbolic Law-of-the-father. The
"écriture blanche" or "writing at degree zero" (Verwaayen 1977, 8)
which corresponds to the desert as a cultural, discursive limit, is
stripped of those modalisations which bind the reader in his/her identification with the story. The hermeneutic blankness which results from
such a laying bare of the discursive nuts and bolts, in a narrative development working away from symbolic codes as it moves forwards,
matches the narrator's desire to "recapture that time from before
writing" (Brossard 1990, 28). Similarly, the dismantling of plot coherence through the absence of a weapon, a gun-shot, a sustained focus
or a motive concerning the scene of Angela Parkin's assassination,
serves to sever threads of logical continuity. The anti-plot of the body
without the murder, the end before the cause, thus works on the symbolic identifications at work in the field of origins – both narrative and
historical. The scene thus represents Brossard's staging and undermining of the way history works in its naturalizing and integrating of
those narrative "plots" it produces.

If the textual figures of "speed", "light", "white", "desert" are some of the text's elaborations of "a movement directed towards an elsewhere", but one "whose characteristics cannot be clearly defined", what is apparent is their subverting of linear plot order, in a trajectory directed at "undermining the apparent stability of the subject positions available in the Symbolic order" (Cameron 1987, 143). The Brossardian signifier thus "defiles" in both senses of the word, since the uncloseable condensations, repetitions and slippages "turn into desire, the effect of language" (143), and in so doing reveal the illusory mastery of the code.

Brossard has, at length, elaborated on an urban politics, the metropolis as a heterogeneous site; a "nervous and erotic system just as the tongue and language are movement in the kissing or speaking mouth" (Brossard 1993, 63). Although the textual figures in *Mauve Desert* are not directly related to urban space they theoretically articulate the same kind of a-symbolic tension in the name of a subjective/discursive/territorial difference. As a counterpoint to the place assigned to women in the Quebec literary tradition of the *roman de la terre* (rural narratives), a novelistic form which is "solid, unified, devoted to the continuation of the Law-of-the-father" (Smart 1988, 90), *Mauve Desert* presents the aesthetic discursive speed, slippage, and fluidity of Brossard's theoretical, urban sites of knowledge. Both open up the prison house of realistic form and the discursive enclosures it articulates. As the narrator claims: "I have opened up roads of sand, I have quenched my thirst and my instinct like so many words in view of the magical horizon ... manoeuvering insanely ... an avalanche of being" (Brossard 1990, 13). These echo the "inroads" that Brossard has made in the discursive bulwark of the Symbolic, in realism's obsessive return to legitimate beginnings, filiation and originality.

As such *Mauve Desert* also strives to release a Quebecois cultural mythology from the image of woman as victim, muse and motherland, as the open wound of a French Canadian trauma of identity. If the novel, like all Brossard's work, attempts to elaborate alternative versions of the female subject's relation to language and culture, the multiple crossings that its translation strategies effect, situate such versions firmly within the conflicted space of a Canadian, national imaginary. The hegemonic recuperations that translation exemplifies in its reliance on stable knowledges – the certainty of "legitimate" origins – is thus here put to the test within the linguistically, and culturally divided, yet politically unified Canadian cultural space.

Geo-political Mappings: Distance and Difference

Aritha van Herk, *Places Far From Ellesmere*: Place, Perception, Self

A map is not *the* territory, but a territory itself. (Robinson and Petchenik cited in van Herk 1992, 57)

The two texts in this section, *Places Far From Ellesmere* and *The Prowler*, could be called Arctic fictions. One is a theorising of a contact between self and place within the context of a voyage to the Canadian Far North, to the island of Ellesmere, the other a meditation on the role of fiction itself in the shaping of identity when the Northern national territory one inhabits is the object of multiple appropriations. Both Aritha van Herk and Kristjana Gunnars examine the links between geo-political interests and discursive configurations. Both writers investigate the thresholds of meaning which open onto alternative spaces, revealing the forces of contradiction at work in any singular version of the self in relation to place. Both thus deal closely with discursive limits and power relations; they are conscious of culture as a conflicted and contested space of vested interests, where both the concept and the reality of "the border" take on particular signification.

Cartography and Ontology

Aritha van Herk, a writer of Dutch origins from Western Canada, identifies cartography as a kind of interpretation, as a generic category exploiting its own rules and codes and not a transparent reflection of a given reality. Her criticism and fiction are ongoing explorations into the relation between place and self – the links between Canadian geography and ontology – and the constraints of both fictional representations and feminine, socio/symbolic representations. Her work is concerned with the "man-made" categories structuring perspectives on place and landscape, and simultaneously with how such representa-

tions include or exclude differences. If Lau's writing seemingly problematizes its own clichéd encodings, as symbolic identifications break
down, van Herk's fiction resolutely focusses on those sites of ambivalence where inside and outside are structured discursively and
open onto an exploration of the female self as "Other".

Engaged in deconstructing both Canadian and masculine perspectives on prairie space and literary representations, van Herk thus
makes claims for a "[d]e-siring" (1992, 79) of national and literary
representations. Not surprisingly, such playing with generic categories
and challenging of their premises, results in a border play of fictional
representation, an exploration of the limits of the Law of the Symbolic.

Thus van Herk's novel, *No Fixed Address*, (already cited in relation
to the grandmother of Goto's *Chorus of Mushrooms* who reworks the
prairie as imaginative territory), similarly remaps Canadian territory.
It revises the quest genre to produce a feminine picaresque narrative
which reinvents the Western scenario of the male adventure hero. In
doing so it questions the epistemological premises linking Canadian
imaginary territory to a masculine logocentric world view.

Places Far From Ellesmere continues the investigation of *No Fixed
Address*, but rather than concentrating on an imaginative revision
within the main character's narratorial perspective, van Herk here
focusses on geographical sites as the centre of consciousness. Thus,
the relation of self to place is challenged from the start, as well as the
inherently subjective perspective which is naturalized as "objective"
in such a relation. She indeed sets out to revise those nineteenth-
century representations of Arctic space which have, in exploration
narratives, given us "the confrontation of the White man with the sublime North often boiling down to a revelation of the individual's stat-
ure" (Omhovère 2002b, 80).

Geographical sites and their cartographic encodings which have
traditionally been intimately linked to feminine representation and
"the troping of the landscape as feminine ... [either] as a comforting
mother or a castrating dangerous femininity" (Mott 1998, 106), are
thus held up to scrutiny in the novel. Both outer and inner perceptions
emerge as belonging to the same problem of language: that of defining
and establishing a stable source of presence.

As the novel's jacket cover illustrates in its collage representation
of a woman "mapped" as an island, whose contours do not exactly
match the mainland, van Herk is here engaging with, in Graham Huggan's words, a "resiting of the traditional 'mimetic fallacy' of cartographic representation" (Huggan 1991, 131). The cover not only

questions the relation of man to map, and the relationship of map to territory, but also poses the problem of women's status in society and representation. In multiple ways the image provokes a reflection on identity in that it challenges "the claim to coherence of cartographic discourse", since maps refer back to "a point of presence whose stability cannot be guaranteed" (Huggan 1991, 128); Jacques Derrida's theorizing of discourse and difference (1978) is here taken up by Graham Huggan for postcolonial ends.

The narrator's locating of the self thus seeks to examine the apparently "natural" relationship between self and place, and, indirectly, between the whole process of naming, identifying and tracing of boundaries which characterized colonial missions and allowed the appropriation of territory. By unhinging identity from its fixed moorings, subjective experience and fictional "reality" here enter into a paradoxical relation of non-coincidence. The reticence to match experience evenly to place, even while putting place at the centre of lived experience, sets up a series of explorations into the relationship between the two. Such explorations allow for epistemological comings and goings which indeed, "in [their] unforeseen associations ... far exceed mimetic reference" (Heim 1999, 140).

In this series of fictional encounters of place as cognitive and subjective space, the narrator's mental map of childhood memories of growing up in the small rural town of Edberg could be seen as an imaginative response to van Herk's own critical statement that a map is "not a tracing of shape but a means of shaping" (van Herk 1992, 58). Place here thus deflects the gaze, returning to the narrator a fractured image that exceeds any comfortable matchings. As such, perceptions on her childhood haunts are not centred in a fixed point of nostalgic return which would ensure a realistic subjective self-presence, but rather disperse the point of focus itself. Place here thus undermines the referential role normally played by "objective" reality as backdrop or setting in the structuring of coherent narrative positions and plots.

When the narrator ponders whether Edberg, lost in the prairies is "an elaborate fabrication" (van Herk 1990, 15) in it "own recitation and inflection" (17) the village is granted status as both interiority and exteriority. The notion of "location" is therefore problematized, it is here neither a point in geography not an index of awareness but a shifting, positional term in which the very modulations or differences are its structuring premises. By extension, the narrator's various explorations into the mappings of the female self onto, and within such locations, simultaneously attest to the non-cohesive premises of such subjecthood. Therefore, Edberg with its dusty streets is a "coppice" of origins but its "desire and return" (13) signal not so much the nostalgia of the narrator returning to the place she grew up, as the laying out of terms of possibility for the structuring of Edberg as a fiction within a project of interpretation. A project which would maintain a steady relationship between cognitive, perceptual, affective and referential data in the shaping of reality, and call the very notion of a stable reference into question. Edberg, in its strategic centering of an "outside world, north, south, passing through/interrupting itself" (16), its overdetermined location a "six square blocks difficult to establish main street" (19), displaces notions of geographical space onto that of subjective perception and thus onto various possible discursive positionings. "Home" is thus here signifying space, as much a moment of f(r)iction within discourse as a place linked to the narrator's past, as the narrator herself conjectures, when she inscribes textual hesitation within a musing on self-location: "How then, do you occupy a place: a site effacing itself, a town dis/appearing, dis/allowed" (29).

The comings and goings of these signifying instances, hovering between presence and absence of verbal form, as the sign "place" negotiates its own location in an unstable textual environment, are part of an investigation into the way we read the past, constructing a viable narrative out of random experience. Such a reading renders a particular moment in time as meaningful from our own particular standpoint, from one of the endless "determinations of the centre" which give our personal narratives their structure. In the narrator's case such a moment is represented by the "Scandinavians [who] ate smelly fish at Christmas ... [who] had TV, although you never watched, instead played upstairs in all the closets. You knew that house as well as your own" (21). Experience as a personal fiction-of-the-self thus maps the place on which it relies to give its fiction ontological validity, to "Centre" its "centre", so to speak. The inscribing of a set of experiential values, sensations and desires makes of Edberg a meaningful, but ultimately provisional instance of subjective place/time.

Contested Spaces: Un-Settling Readings

If *Places Far From Ellesmere* calls for dissonance as the premise of the locating of selfhood, such an invitation to differential readings challenges not only perceptions of reading as truth value, but also questions the nation as a stable code. The narrative seeks to "site" Canada through a focus on its territory as divided up and carved out within a network of imaginary visions and appropriations passing as

geography. The linear account of peaceful settlement and development is shown to be in fact one interpretation within multiple possible
readings of Canada's beginnings. The disappropriations of Native
lands and the erasure of their culture which settlement engendered is
here invoked through urban planning lines and limits drawn across the
(still open) debate on colonisation/settlement in all its contradictions.
The narrator insists on those dividing lines and distancing technologies of civilisation which have mapped out urban spaces across the
weave of the mountains and the prairie. Edmonton, the city of "long
division", the "city that will divide you from the country" (43), thus
opens up distances and differences within singular representations of
community and national identity. Cartography and town-planning are
seen as so many mathematical encodings which enacted the city's
beginnings in the nineteenth century: "The four great highways leading from Winnipeg, the great Bow River grazing country ... the termi-
nus of the CP telegraph line, the North-West mail route"(44). The
narrator's statement "You might as well start here" precedes her
question "How do you start a life in Edmonton?" (45) The reason for
settlement resides therefore in the performing of settlement itself; in
its textualisation. If "Edmonton is a reading, an act of text" (47), its
discursive syntax is that of vested interests: the economic and colonial
drives for territory are shown as belying any simple interpretation of
Canada as an empty, (female or Native) space waiting (and willing) to
be "taken" peacefully.

For when representing Edmonton as:"a fort(ress) set up to
trade/skin Indians. The Hudson's Bay Company holding its own centuries later" (43), the narrator underscores the continuity of exploita-
tion as the most persistent trace of the settling process. Likewise, as
Graham Huggan states out, "the drive west, symbolized by
Mackenzie's expeditions in the eighteenth century, may well have
been geographically oriented, but it was economically motivated". As
he continues, stressing the role of cartography itself in settlement; "by
helping to implement policies of territorial negotiation, appropriation,
and expansion, nineteenth-century surveys became indispensable
agents of the colonizing process" (1994, 36-7).

The fr)ictions of beginnings, the play of ideological, economic and
human development are therefore represented as so many discursive
thresholds. A narrative grammar is elaborated whereby the "long division" of Edmonton, and the "declensions" of Calgary (van Herk 1990,
43, 62), are the mathematical/syntactic benchmarks of the narrator's
apprenticeship of fitting self into difference, of sharing the rhetorical
jumps and swerves of those places she binds to and bonds with. As

she makes her way into the codes of college and work, the textual play
of difference also signifies her own position as subject in the world:
"Long division: what you were never good at, ... You set up the equation, begin with a thick-stemmed landlady who rustles through your
closets when you are in classes" (45). Similarly, contested and con-
testing spaces are textually drawn out, and their boundary limits are
topographical, economic and historical: "How much/how long/how
big?" is the narrator's musing on the "declension of money" (65),
while "Calgary as quadrant ... quartering the city NW/NE/SE/SW"
(70), puts differentiation and definition at the centre of both the textual and the cartographic enterprise. If town planning is here a metaphor of the rational, logic of development and conquest in the
construction of Canada, it echoes van Herk's own words: "Clearly
mapping, like language, is creation more than representation, and so it
is not illogical to think of fiction as cartography" (van Herk 1992, 58).

Yet as Edmonton and Calgary emerge in van Herk's representation
as an effect of discourse, the prevalent word plays she uses posit a
juggling with this cartography of conquest and a tampering with its
fixed ontological limits. Calgary, "the city a centre of spokes, *em-
penned*" (66, emphasis mine), is thus both defined, encircled, historicized by the "[t]eepee rings, medicine wheels, effigies" marking
out the trace of the first inhabitants and also written (*penned*) into
existence as the text of settlement. Likewise, the "[f]reeways [which]
stop abruptly" (73) at the edge of hills speak of civilisation as the haphazard phrasing in a discourse of city space which rises and tumbles
"in a fringe of crumbling asphalt" (73). Such images are testimony to
the postmodern provisonality of culture itself in its urban representations. For, when the narrator exclaims: "Who can find you here, a
clumsy bawling beast in the centre of a web of thread, a cat's cradle of
encapturement" she pits the contemporary "scene" of Calgary in its
speed and condensation of space/time co-ordinates, its jostling codes
and labyrinthine shopping malls, against the "fossils of lost centuries"
(74) or the "sharp edge of Shaganappi coulee" (73). The narratives of
colonisation and Western invention, mapped onto the First Nations
traces of nomadism, thus produce a dense matrix of namings and re-
namings, of construction and destruction. Canadian national identity is
here, it seems, best apprehended as discontinuity: as beginnings, mul-
tiplications and thresholds.

Self-identity in such space is rendered in the wavering of rhetoric
itself, in the hinging and unhinging properties of prefixes, underlining
the way language's internal logic can be interrupted to disrupt the
transparent flow of meaning. Thus, the incisions carved into

"[d]is/criminate" and "fore/shortened", affect and "infect" interpretation, displaying syntactically what the narrative as a whole examines: the way in which "cultural and political identity are constructed through a process of alterity", as an "uncomfortable, disturbing practice of survival and supplementarity – between art and politics, past and present" (Bhabha 1994, 175). Such a narratorial focus which takes language both as its object and its instrument, strives to resituate the disparate historical claims to recognition. The territorial precedence of the First Nations is set in a counter-discursive relation to the globalizing abstractions of Western economic interests. Thus, the description the: "Sarcee woman in the Co-op store turning over *running* shoes (related to *Deerfoot*), her hair *knifing* over her face. You *edge* past her, but always want to touch that *encarved* posture" (van Herk 1990, 68, emphasis mine), presents the play of cultural f(r)ictions which emerge in the interstices of meaning as an effect of language itself.

Furthermore, such embedding of history as a semantic and linguistic trace is also a means of questioning our naturalizing perceptions on landscape, revealing the encodings constituting our experience of nature. As van Herk has commented regarding the Canadian West: "The prairie cannot escape the image that has been imposed on it. Art stages place and place shapes art, but here, it is as though the signified is in bondage to the signifier" (van Herk 1992, 140). The narrative, through its defamiliarizing strategies, seeks to undo that iconographic pact and to jostle our expectations of authoritative vision. The description of the "devouring edges" of hills "stitching themselves into the ground", and the "outskirts of outskirts outskirted" (van Herk 1990, 71), forge a gap within iconography, unstitch the seams which bind landscape into a coherent textual representation of Canadian nationhood.

The concept of "Canada" is worked on, and through, as a collective and individual discursive space. Both contentious and unequal it becomes completely entangled in those slippery identifications which reveal themselves within the novel's textual play of distance and difference. Resisting any reading which would fold place into a historical narrative of origins, the particular contentions that become "declensions" in van Herk's narrative syntax of urban labyrinth, jagged mountain outcrop, or rural town, are so many questionings on just what a narrative of origins could be. Between metropole and rural territory, the narrator's beginnings and her narratives of development, writing emerges as a particuarly Canadian engagement with the rhetoricity of place, with the need to map the self, even as mapping implies the presence and positioning of the mapper.

Mapping the Mapper

As Shirley Neuman has stated, the island Ellesmere as "tabula rasa" marks the narrator's final destination as a "contestatory"site (Neuman 1996, 230). That Ellesmere has been been analysed as a representation of woman as island which "replicates the traditional portrayal of the North as a blank space ready to be used for one's own purpose and narrative", or that van Herk has "exploited the North by [her] literary importation of Anna Karenina" (Aritha van Herk citing criticism she received on the novel from "a very well-known northern scholar": 1998, 86), seems, to my mind, to be a misconstruing of the overall drive of the novel. For, what the narrator's trajectory through the sites of her past and present has played with, and opened out, are the fault lines in the myths of mapping as a corollary of, and a metaphor for, a certain version of harmonious settlement; a version of a virgin land, waiting to be named and given an identity. Seen from this angle the novel focusses on both the phallocentric and the imperialistic appropriations of Canadian geographical, economic and imaginary space.

Furthermore, if van Herk has dubbed the work a "geograficitione", thus underlining the interweaving of fiction and geography as a process of, and reflection on representation, this ultimately *critical* project informs the whole novel. This is not so much a quest towards an alternative, ideologically freed, "essential" feminine landscape (with all its attendant theoretical deadends), but rather a strategic engagement with culture as discursive space, and with the means of its reading/re-reading/unreading. The "virgin" territory of Ellesmere could thus be seen, not as an implicit erasure of the "evidence of hunters' camps from over four thousand years ago" (Neuman 1996, 223), but as part of the final move of van Herk's exercise in "remapping the mapper" (See van Herk 1992, 65); as if she were turning the lens around to focus the positioning that realism both masks by its function, and reveals by its presence as language – I am borrowing van Herk's own concept here in a different but nonetheless related way (see 1992, 54-68). This constitutes a perspective which implicitly posits a subjective positioning in any "reading" of the world, and the "world" as an effect of that reading; the fact that the "I" experiencing can never be identical with the "I" imaged in the social symbolic, that "identity" is, in sum, a fiction. Van Herk plays with the chimera of stable subjective positionings – which language itself elaborates and holds in place –

through such strategies as shifting pronouns and disrupted syntax. She does so to constantly interrogate the position from which the subject speaks, and as corollary, the possibility of a coherent, female positioning in discourse. As Neuman says, the autobiographical mode of the narrative is "about sending oneself to oneself in a different writing" (Neuman 1996, 222), thus underlining the contradiction at the centre of female self-representation. The series of subjective, implicitly gendered splittings operating throughout the narrative, in its focus on what interpretation "naturalizes", is crystalized in the collage of the cover mentioned before. The "woman as island" of Ellesmere seemingly pulled away from the mainland which, at first view, she should "naturally" fit into, could be interpreted as a cartographic/rhetorical rendering of the "map" of society in general. Ellesmere, seen in this light in its "awayness so thoroughly truant" (van Herk 1990, 77), represents an unlawful dream and dilation, effacement and contradiction; that mythical "virgin" North is tactically manoeuvred and rewritten as an extreme limit where the "[w]hite nights" (90) signal a zero point of total (critical) exposure. In this context, Marlene Goldman's Deleuzian interpretation of Ellesmere as a "deterritorialized" site of a "nonhierarchized body" seems particularly apt (1993, 34), since the presence of Tolstoy's heroine in the foreground in Ellesmere will bring the question of "un-reading" to bear as narrative strategy.

For the narrator's reading of *Anna Karenina* in Ellesmere is a rereading of Tolstoy's fictional practice, taking to task his masculinist interpretation of "Woman" as "Other"; the way he, through the character of Levin, "mis/reads the outward appearance of all women. ... he separates them into the finite categories of fallen and unfallen (van Herk 1990, 104)". Yet if the narrator seeks to free Anna from her misreading, the heroine is inversely the path of access to Ellesmere for the narrator. For the latter, in her own reading of Anna's misreading, discovers an access to an altered perceptive horizon. The Russian heroine's enclosure within Tolstoy's text provides a liminal point of contact, an "entrance" *into* and not *overlooking* Ellesmere since: "... re/reading her, in Ellesmere a/new, reading her whole, you can re/write her too" (83): I am borrowing van Herk's conceptual striving to find the means to fracture that prairie metaphor of "vantage" and "vision", one which she states is "impossibly male, without entrance" (1992, 141). Although Ellesmere represents a different geographical, geopolitical space, it shares the same epistemological and ontological pre-occupations that govern van Herk's theorizing of literary and cartographic renderings of the prairie.

As both subject and object then, the narrator and the heroine merge in a fiction of f(r)ictions, which break down ontological barriers and allow for the narrator's own "textualisation" as she slips into the pages of the Russian narrative. Its nineteenth-century, teleological plot thus crosses over into the narrator's own space of beginnings; Tolstoy's narrative "train", becomes "a version of train, that grubby dayliner from Edberg suddenly enormous, bearing down on history and fiction" (83). This folding of one ontological space into the other represents the culmination of van Herk's ficto/critical, crypto/f(r)ictional venture to the edge; the Arctic threshold becomes a mode of transforming the literary, culturally gendered, "Other" into a rewriting of the self. Seen in this light, van Herk's strategic northern site is both a delighting in, and "dilating" of the Canadian North "of objective and scientific account"; it is a critical "entrance" into the "scape" which she cites as a term whose "archaic meaning ... is to escape" (van Herk 1992, 140).

What, to my mind, prevents the island representation from falling back into the trap of an idealized, essentialized, feminine space is precisely this critical gesture pushing the encodings to their limits within a strategy of rereading. Through this critical journey in several stages, Ellesmere as Arctic space is not the metaphor of a feminine "already-read" vista, but an imaginary horizon, or "scape/escape", opened within the social/political/phallocentric world view staged by Tolstoy, and by which Tolstoy's text is put to work in its own unreading. The thresholds which emerge from the narrator's self-reading through reading Anna, an operation which effectively rereads Tolstoy, serves to envisage alterity itself as a dynamic enunciatory possibility.

Geografictione thus represents a "fictioneering" move in the Arctic zone hitherto reserved for male pioneering, an epistemological, female-centred exploration in the "kingdom of the male virgin" (90-9); van Herk is here speaking on literary "mappings" of the Canadian (far) West, but as I have attempted to demonstrate, her questioning of modes of representation of the West is equally valid for a (far) North as adventure myth and nostalgic reference of lost origins (see 1992, 90-9). The concept of *geografictione* likewise strives to approach that structuring difference of subjecthood itself which gives onto what are revealed to be the "fictions" of stable presence, enbedded in cultural representation.

The complex, theoretical and imaginative nature of such an investigation, scripting, as van Herk's neologism *geografictione* implies, the encounter between fictional words and the landscape it seeks to represent, does not in the final analysis seek to measure subjective to objective reality. The narrative seeks precisely to question the nature and measure the value of such an objective reality, both in terms of what is at stake for women, and for a Canadian identity in the face of its multiple political and territorial reconstructions through exploration, conquest and appropriation.

Kristjana Gunnars, *The Prowler*: Territorial Rights, Textual Ways

It is a relief not to be writing a story. Not to be imprisoned by character and setting (Gunnars 1989, section 3).

If we turn to Kristjana Gunnars' *The Prowler*, we realize the problematizing of what constitutes objective reality is also central to the novel; the vexed relation between words and the world is foregrounded. But here we could say that the "geography" implicit in van Herk's *geografictione* is a structuring absence in Gunnars' text. The geopolitical forces shown to be at work in the representation of the narrator's hybrid Danish/Icelandic cultural heritage seem to subsume the very notion of national territory within a narration that underlines the exigencies of superpowers and their disdain for, and occupation of, strategic Northern outposts. *The Prowler* thus, as Diana Brydon aptly puts it, uses "the recurrent postcolonial metaphor of the colony as the empire's garbage dump ... powerless to refuse others' refuse, what others have refused" (Brydon 1991, 200).

The "prowler" of the title has multiple resonances in the narrative, as a sleuth in search of an adequate fiction through which to express her complex territorial/personal/political identity, the self-conscious aspect of this discursive stalking giving the novel its metafictional dimension, and as a reading position which will be discussed later. The theme of the novel also seems to signal the "murder" of a country, a territorial spoliation where the "corpse" cannot be fully identified. Since Iceland as a nation state uncontaminated by others' historical imperatives is portrayed, in Gunnars' text, as ultimately unrepresentable. We are left with the impression that adequate representation would require a vision outside, or above, or beyond the massive and violent expropriations which the novel stages, a vision capable of proposing a "before" of such expropriation. Therefore, unlike van Herk's narrative of the North, which elaborates a feminine reappropriation of meaning through the symbolic encounter with Arctic space, *The Prowler* seems to fall prey to, wrestle with, but also figuratively "stalk" the multiple fractures and incoherencies that constitute the "endless discriminations of difference" (198) of the history of Iceland.

Contact Zones

As the narrator of *The Prowler* states, she is a "White Inuit", an appelation which, according to Diana Brydon invokes the Icelanders' status as "privileged by race and underprivileged by location". (198) The text will go on to explore what it means to live between identities as the narrator experiences the hardships and nonsensical reality of an American occupation and the problems of a shared Icelandic/Danish heritage. Brydon has commented the see-sawing between the sense of an authentic identity on the one hand, and the cross-cultural impetus of the narrative in its multiple dislocations on the other. As she states, the narrator's role as "border-prowler" evacuates from the text the notion of "[c]ultural purity" (198). What the narrative does do, in its ultimate refusal of a mythic rewriting of history, or an envisaging of a symbolic reinvestment in language itself, is to deny the possibility of representing the reality of dispossession in any causally logical way. Instead, the fields of subjective perception and narrative focalisation provide ways to displace geopolitical borders onto the field of rhetorical slippage. Thus the workings of power relations can connect with the domain of human relations and suffering. For example, the narrator speaks of the possibility of "a murder" which would happen "somewhere on that American base" and veers off to a meditation on naming as a way of ordering personal experience: "Much later in life I contrived a poetics of naming" (Gunnars 1989, sections 51-2). Méira Cook analyses such displacements as "an exchange circuit" in "a shuffle text" where shifting identifications signify the slippages of amatory discourse, a discourse where the "lover" is "constructed alternately as prowler, writer, and reader" (Cook 1988, 20). Through the privileging of perception, desire and loss, the global issues of geopolitics are inscribed in the local, and the personal and Gunnars, through her deployment of postmodern strategies, persistently refuses the lure of synthesizing logic and plot. Instead, diverse topics, semantic areas, subjective positionings enter into unexpected associations: "I became aware that for us in the North dreams never did come true. … I will never be Japanese. … Dreams are the closed mussels lying among the stones in the fjord. … It was a country that needed geothermal energy so there could be industry and growth (sections 38, 40). The logic which unites them is that of the superpowers' failure in logic – to bridge the gap between transnational manoeuvering and the individuals whose interests they are ostensibly "protecting". In its fore-grounding of our cognitive limits, and its proposing of alternative, personal and anecdotal sets of associations, Gunnars' text recalls Michaels' *Fugitive Pieces*. To the extent that this is a fiction of the North representing a nation's submitting to the strategic interests of other nations, it provides an interface with the concerns of Canadian First Nations and their claims for recognition (ones which as far as the Inuits are concerned, have finally resulted in territorial boundaries and self-government). Gunnars' narrative therefore indirectly raises crucial Canadian problems of individual and collective agency.

In the narrative's deployment of novel connections we are in fact confronted with a constant challenge to any attempt on our part to construct any easy categories or form judgements. Rather the narrator confronts different positionings, interrogates a world order founded in contradiction and incoherence:

> I read the history of Iceland's involvement in World War II. One morning during the war I read, people woke up to find they were occupied by the British. This was to preempt the possible arrival of the Germans. British soldiers flooded the streets. The radio spoke English. ... Then just as suddenly the British were gone, and people woke up to find they were occupied by the Americans. (Gunnars 1989, section 45)

> Reading *Morgunbladid*, the Icelandic daily, I saw the population of the island was being reassured. The American Base, it said, is not a nuclear base. Some months later in Canada I happened upon an American military map. Iceland, it showed, is a nuclear base (section 30).

But not only are the post-war geopolitical interests of the Americans and Russians set in contradiction, but the narrator's personal history is also caught between an Icelandic and a Danish heritage, her positioning in society shown to be a mobile hierarchy of values according to the company she keeps: "In my father's country I was known as the dog-day girl, a monarchist, a Dane. ... In my mother's country other kids circled me haughtily on their bicycles. They whispered among each other on the street corners that I was a white Inuit, a shark-eater" (section 16).

Furthermore, the dividing of the narrative into short sections, instead of providing the continuity of pagination, structurally mirrors the gaps in causality of history that the narrative thematizes, preventing any sustained focus and creating points of contact between diverse discourses. Thus metonymy creates unexpected analogies, rendering within a seemingly arbitrarily dispersed form, the equally arbitrary nature of Iceland's history. Haphazard incidents are juxtaposed, representing the spoliation of national territory through the spoliation of its inhabitants; the violation of political rights is exposed through the violence threatening those most vulnerable, yet without any narratorial intervention to confer authority: "This was the country where people died of starvation … Yet the shores were full of mussels. … People refused to eat the mussels. I did not like the American servicemen who sometimes came to our house. … It is a nothing memory. A non-memory" (sections 35-40). The unexpected associations between deprivation and self-privation, occupation and absence (of memory) create a fragile texture, one "constantly under (de)construction" (Beautell 2000, 31-2). Thus not only does the narrative displace the political onto the personal but the fracturing and multiplicity which characterize it, and the narrator's relinquishing of efforts to create a causal chain of plausibility, make it difficult to identify any unified "authentic" narratorial position. Precisely this deploying of "the notion of identity as a *strategy* undermining the very logic of identity" (32, emphasis mine) makes of *The Prowler* an interesting instance of the continuing redefinition of postcolonial subjectivity. For if Black or Asian writers' integration in Canada is often tied up with crucial questions of racial discrimination as well as cultural difference – questions leading them to rediscover a past in order to define their place as Canadian subjects within their particular cultural heritages, Gunnars' text takes up different options. The ongoing conflict between a claim for recognition of a heritage culture on the one hand and on the other hand the breaking through the limits that relegation to the role of the racialized "Other" can produce, does not seem to be the issue here. Gunnars' own status as White Canadian immigrant (and therefore not subject to the prejudice of the "visibly different") is a partial explanation. Yet the narrator (and Gunnars), do have conflicting cultural loyalties to contend with, but they are ones which preclude any single point of "authentic" reference with regard to identity. For the narrative's representation of Iceland as a subservient colony to Danish domination (whereas both Iceland and Denmark are part of Gunnars' own heritage in relation to a "Canada" which ghosts the text) raises the question of where – on what affective, cultural grounds – a "centred", or even imaginatively "recentred" identity could be founded. By extension, it would seem that no unitary, binding association between subjecthood, language, and a single "mother" country could be valid for Gunnars. Therefore, the multiplicity which informs the narrative, and the evacuating of any mythical dimension or any sustained imaginative "retrieval", while at the same time putting the whole question of affiliation and the role of language in the foreground, seem to express an experience of identity as an inner border, a linguistic and affective threshold rather than a fixed point of attachment.

The result is that *The Prowler* engages, like van Herk's text, with exploring the way representation itself is ultimately an appropriation, because always filtered through a subjective positioning, always complicit with vested interests. The narrative, through its multiplying of discordant, non-synchronous representations and positionings, emphasizes the provisional nature of political discourses; it multiplies and thus undermines the diverse "vantage points" (van Herk 1992, 141-2) occupied by the Danish, American and Russians in Iceland's history, but in the same breath it also shows the effects of those occupations on the narrator herself. The uncontrollable nature of politics and its effects are often given to us as a fracture, as a non-coincidence between appearances and reality, needs and their satisfactions. The American CARE packages to the population are shown to be "full of useless objects" (Gunnars 1989, section 9), instead of the fruit and vegetables they need, just as the narrator's hair colour means she is taken for a Russian by her Danish peers. Likewise the narrator's view on Americans changes from distrust to friendship when she herself goes to the United States, and the privileges she enjoys in a Danish boarding-school are due to her "one-time appearance on American television" (section 65). Misinterpretations and reinterpretations thus serve to construct the narrator's reality, one which she overtly cites as fiction:

> "Some Icelandic novels make no sense? They are not meant to make sense. They go nowhere, refuse to grasp reality, say there is no reality. Potentially there is no reality. My father's people have always known that potentially they do not exist" (section 30).

Yet, as Daniel Coleman points out, the narrator's fractured existence, her "flux of divided loyalties and affiliations" nonetheless affords her "a kind of liberatory agency" (Coleman 1994, 22).

Conflicted Voice; Voicing Conflict

With its emphasis on the deferred truth value of political and social reality, and on self-conscious fictional devices, *The Prowler* is of course drawing our attention to the vexed relation between them; the constant border-crossings between domains implicitly admits of "a situation where the writer, the reader and the text meet within an entire historical, social, and political, as well as literary, context" (Hutcheon 1988, 16). It is as though the narrator's own voice became a conflictual territory where differences and distances are inscribed.

Narrative voice, a function of textual process, thus registers the shifts and manoeuvres of a world which does not reach any settled, unified status. The unresolvable conflicts of geopolitical interests in the Arctic and the absence of an adequate representation of Icelandic nationhood are in this way displaced onto the terrain of the text's discursive authority.

To this end, *The Prowler* deploys a first-person narrative perspective through which to locate the extremely fragmented universe we are being invited to actively participate in, and simultaneously, through this fractured perspective, undermines any authoritative vision. One thinks once again of the term "autobiographics" invoked in relation to Evelyn Lau's journal, since the voice of Gunnars' text also informs us of the multiple discourses from which it emerges rather than to construct a seamless world for our readerly identification. This voice signals in fact, often overtly, a "reading practice" (Gilmore 1998, 184) rather than being a mediator to plot or character, and it continually displaces the terms on which our reading takes place. We are constantly put in the position of asking ourselves not "who" is the subject of speech, for there is no ambivalence as to the narrator's identity, but rather "from where" this voice is speaking, from what location in a world view or "vantage point" on a world. In so much as the narrator shifts from self-questioning to philosophizing on the nature of the story: "[y]et the story intrudes. Where did it begin?" to personal reminiscences: "my father was always going far away in airplanes and bringing home Toblerone chocolates" (section 6), the value of the speaking "I" varies accordingly. When the narrator deliberates on her own status as narrator: "It is a relief not to be writing a story", or on the status of story-telling itself: "All stories are romances. Detective stories, spy thrillers" (sections 52-3), the constructedness of the "I" is foregrounded and, by extension, so is the ideological aspect of such an "authentic" individual consciousness. Gunnars' voice thus problematizes the whole question of fictional representation as appropriation and of political appropriations as unstable and fictitious representations.

If the narrator emphasizes her role as a shaper of perceptions and foregrounds the collusion between politics and representation, she also "prowls" the borders of language as a system inventing rather than reflecting reality. The reiterated use of the syntactic form "there is/are": "[t]here are some moments that seem to be live ones"; "[t]here are things we know long before we know them" (sections 2, 19), which linguistically both predicate existence and the independence of that existence (in that such linguistic forms create a semantic break,

are independent of what has gone before), has the effect of both engendering an identity itself from the matrix of language and expressing the relation of difference which that engendering produces. Thus,
in its reiteration of forms which create breaking points and yet simultaneously seek to establish an identity, the narrative is constantly engaging in thresholds of knowledge, enacting and re-enacting
signifying instances when identity emerges as difference. Likewise the
narrator's stating of opinions: "[i]t is a world that never was", or "[i]t
is a relief to be under no obligation", and use of demonstrative forms:
"[t]his is the voice that sits by hospital beds" (sections 23, 28, 101),
veer away from continuity, from joining parts together in a logical
pattern of events, and yet seek to express what John Lent has called
"an intense subjectivity". As he states, the quality of voice and the
fragmented form makes it seem as if the "entire text [were] delivered
offstage, relieved of official stories" (1991, 106), a type of narration
which (along with the narrator herself), he is reluctant to attribute
exclusively to a specifically feminine consciousness. Yet, the quotation from Marguerite Duras' *The Lover* which provides an epigraph to
the narrative: "The story of my life doesn't exist. Does not exist.
There's never any center to it" (Gunnars 1989, epigraph), and Gunnars' own comments to the effect that women are to some degree always immigrants (see Lent 1991, 107), nonetheless point to crucial
questions of how discourse positions us in the world, and how all
"outsiders" (women as well as immigrants) share problems of representation. We could situate the type of consciousness expressed in *The
Prowler* not only as a poetical aesthetics but as a poetics of the subject, playing on and around the paradox motivating subjecthood.
I mean that part of consciousness which is irretrievably lost to the
subject and which enables entry into the social order, thus inscribing
loss as the very condition of desire.

   We could say then that the subject-in-play at the centre of Gunnars'
strategies is an experimentation with that instance when subjective
"failure" initiates the desire which conditions representation but which
representation cannot satisfy. As such the subject-in-play in *The
Prowler*, in all its multiple entries and exits – the blanks and still-
nesses, desire and loss which the narrative produces – is less, to my
mind, the "offstage" voice of an "unofficial point of view" than the
(playful) staging, or staging (as narratorial play), of the paradox of
subjecthood itself, one by which "off" and "on-stage", inside and outside, are the shaky terms on which representation(s) (political, social
and discursive) maintain their coherence. This is the source of, and
grounds for Gunnars' intensely poetic and epistemological investiga-

tion of subjectivity. It is an investigation which stages the same set of questions which haunt the social/narrative text of both women and immigrants.

Furthermore, as Lent so rightly intimates, the deconstructive drive of *The Prowler* could have congealed into an alternative orthodoxy if Gunnars had "become too self-conscious about the theoretical game she was playing" (106). *The Prowler* does not take off into a spiralling self-reflexive, metanarrative; it throws out threads but does not sustain any of its strategic forays, thus relinquishing any systematic recourse or commitment to one discourse or another. The narrative thus retains an urgency and a kind of pathos. For the narrative creates a link between the abandonment of any belief in any political cure for the ills of Iceland, and the literal scars on the community body caused by such political disdain for the nation. She emphasizes the gap between supposedly beneficial official policies, and the traces left on the Icelanders through the "turberculosis, leprosy, scurvy, polio" that are the "national inheritance" (Gunnars 1989, section 36), and which testify to the occupiers' lack of empathy and commitment. Moreover, such abandoning of any ethical, affective responsability by the colonisers is mirrored in Gunnars' refusal of any one focalizing position within the narrative itself. For dispersal seems to inhabit the narrative as its causal premises, as the narrator's intermittent relating of her sister's anorexia, her own experience of hunger and ill-health and the ludicrous inequation between back-breaking work and the few "dirty radishes carried home to [her] mother's kitchen" (section 26), all challenge the very notion of a common identity to be founded within a national body politic. We are confronted with a narrator who "drops" her voice, cutting short the threads she throws out, changing directions, posing questions, and making statements which challenge, not our ability to make sense of them (for there is no syntactic scrambling here), but rather our ability to attribute reasonable causes, to give reasonable answers to the questions thrown up by the narrative, or to place them within schemas we know and understand.

An Ethics of Reading

Although the intertextual allusions to James Joyce and Günter Grass, the fractured aspect of the narrative, and the intrusions of a self-conscious narrator reflecting on the process of fiction, itself all blur boundaries between text and reader, the aim of such strategies is not, to my mind, to establish a horizon of ever-receding meaning at the centre of the reading process. On the contrary, despite the scattered form, the meditation on the nature of fiction that *The Prowler* affords, and the challenges to rational logic as a way of making sense of the world, the dialogue between text and reader in its multiplication of differences indeed sets up, "a 'carnival' of longing" as Lent so aptly puts it (Lent 1991, 106). This ethical drive for some kind of truth which weaves its way through the fiction and metafictional commentary, comes from the function of reading promoted as process but also as critical practice, which informs the novel as a whole; a process and practice which stems from a paradoxical impulse, filtered through the lens of contemporary critical theory, to use the concept of reading in order to undo reading. Such a logic stems from the acceptation that interpretation gets us further, not nearer to the heart of things, and that the "heart of things" – reality itself – is constructed. Thus the narrator tells us: "Words are not what they signify. We confuse the signifier with the signified" (Gunnars 1989, section 52). One function of the "prowlers" in the text is then that of dismantling the conditions on which we read fiction and reality, and critical theory is brought to bear as a lever on these constructions, undoing the plot's progression, working to deliver the text from its interpretations. As we are told: "When we recognize that all our stories are pretense, we run out of enemies. When we run out of enemies all we have left is love. ... A story that does not desire pretense must incorporate its metastories" (section 55).

But of course such is the nature of language and representation that the quest taken up by the multiple "prowlers", including us, the readers, who are drawn into the game, is essentially an impossible one. Just as we cannot back out of the symbolic order, except at the cost of psychic disintegration, so the domain of language and representation is conditioned by, and maintains the desire which it can never fulfill: to get to the heart of things, to reveal "being" instead of "meaning" and thus rejoin the lost source of complete presence. But it is of course, as Méira Cook points out, this subjective split which triggers desire, and enables "love" to emerge from "a profound failure of language" in the narrative (Cook 1988, 21). "Prowling" can then only give rise to more "prowlers" and this in a way is what the novel does in its constant promoting of reading positions: positing the narrator as author/reader, the reader as colonizer, the writer as theorist, the theorist as guardian of reading rights, and institutions as promoters of readings:

> There are always other stories, metastories, about which we have made an industry
> (Gunnars 1989, section 56).

It was James Joyce who said: the reader wants to steal from the text. The reader aspires to be a thief (section 59).

The novel I at one time intended to write rejected itself. It began to talk about its own genesis instead. The story disappeared. In its place there was another story, an unexpected story. A great surprise (section 63).

The narrative's constant searching for the limits to representation takes on then the aspect of a desire, and that of a design, woven around the responsibility of reading (in all its critical inferences) as an ethical practice; it draws a boundary against the reader's appropriation of easy stories, his role as passive consumer, but also by extension, against imperialistic and geo-political appropriations masking self-interest as benefaction. We are given to understand that the presence of "prowlers", challenging our unmediated access to the narrative world, cannot resolve problems of identity but only create more differences, more "contaminations": "I decided to join the prowler in the compilation of puzzle pieces. ... The project was to clarify the picture. ... But we had rough seas, and one morning I found the tediously arranged picture on the floor, again in a shambles. No one had the stamina to begin it again" (section 108).

Yet, these differences or "contaminations" are, as Brydon points out, a form of identity founded in provisionality itself, a strategy to "confuse the categorizers" (Tostevin cited in Brydon 1991, 198). One could add that such a strategy serves here to counter the type of colonial, political and economic "contamination" which the novel also thematizes.

The cognitive spaces which are opened up through all the narrative juxtapositions and realignments – the mixing of fields of emotion and perception with those of self-reflexive commentary – are in constant relation with an ethics of reading the text (and life). The emphasis on mobile subjective positioning that the play between reader, narrator and author produces, is linked to the way each section affords a different perspective but nonetheless privileges point of view over plot. The deconstructive drive in the narrative, and the theoretical apparatus informing this drive, are contained and channeled within the local experiences of the narrator. The major questions on language, politics, and the destiny of the North as strategic dumping ground, are contained within the situated, embodied (Braidotti 1994, 14), texture of the narrative. (Rosi Braidotti's definition of embodiment relies on the postulate that the "truth of the subject is always between self and society"). *The Prowler* does not overtly explicate or promote a set of values but, through the deconstructed form, and sustainedly subjective perspective, maintains a line of force, one which supports Braidotti's statement that since "language is the medium and site of constitution of the subject, it follows that it is also the cumulated symbolic capital of our culture", a "process of negotiation between layers, sedimentations, registers of speech, frameworks of enunciation" (14).

Gunnars' narrative portrays this process of mediation and negotiation through language in its engagement with politics, a negotiation constantly channeled through a subjectively situated narrative focus. Likewise the personal fragments constantly reinvent an itinerary of experience for the narrator. For the repositionings she adopts are more a set of traces than a continuity. They situate this reading practice, or ethics, within a schema representative of Braidotti's definition of identity as "a retrospective notion", in that our "desires are that which evade us in the very act of propelling us forth, leaving as the only indicator of who we are, the traces of where we have already been – that is to say, of what we have already ceased to be" (14).

The set of traces presented to us and which invite us in as participants of this mobile identity-construction thus works not only to divest the narrative of metastories, but also to divest us of ours, to register *The Prowler*'s subject under construction/deconstruction as an operation that concerns us as subjects, that taps into that shared "symbolic capital" of which language is a repository:

> All the memories gathered in the text are sorry ones. The text acknowledges its own sorrow. It does not seek an apology for its own transparency. When we were bathing in the fjord, the barrack-girl and I, an American soldier suddenly appeared behind the rocks. ... I've lost my watch. Would you help me find it? (Gunnars 1989, section 80)

Such traces mobilize our affective capacity in that they also touch upon in the reader precisely those (already mentioned) "desires which evade us in the very act of propelling us forth", those imaginary identifications which we call upon fiction to satisfy and which *The Prowler* awakens.

I would like to propose further that Kristjana Gunnars' own status as subject, her dual linguistic and cultural heritage, and her choice of a third one, Canada (which recalls the "third" as the place of difference itself in Lacanian terms) directly inform *The Prowler*. As Cameron says: "the structures of differentiation ... of language, ... function as a third term defining the relation of the subject and an other". (Cameron 1987, 142). The extreme critical distance taken from a controlling realistic point of view, the constant return to a structuring identity which is incomplete and in process, the refusal of value judgements, and metadiscourses on the nature of reality, all signal an extreme awareness that "[T]here are no mother tongues, just linguistic sites one takes her/his starting point from" (Braidotti 1994, 13). Such a statement is not a promoting of a cynical relativism denying allegiances to a given culture but an ethical stance which precisely describes the situated – both socially and symbolically – politics, that *The Prowler*, to my mind, espouses. One could provide a gloss for the novel in Braidotti's theoretical outcry against the chimera of a unified subject: "I am struck by the gesture which binds a fractured self to the performative illusion of unity, mastery, self-transparence. I am amazed by the terrifying stupidity of that illusion of unity, and by its incomprehensible force" (13).

The Prowler does not offer any answers to community dispersals or cultural dislocation, or the role of the Arctic in geopolitical scenarios, but does provide alternative figurations for such dislocations. If the complex internal negotiations of the narrator's cultural hybridity means there is no sense of retrieval or reinvention of an "authentic" cultural identity, there is an intense investigation into the forms that dislocated, hybrid, or migrant identities can take without compromise, without selling out to an "illusion of unity" wherever such illusions spring from. Such imaginary figurations are thus another perspective on the type of theoretical investigations into subjectivity and its multiple locations within culture which feminists like Braidotti are concerned with. Such a perspective concerns developing imaginative figures for a cross-cultural subjectivity that promote a critical awareness of thresholds and multiplicity as a personal, but also ethical relation to the world.

Genre and Gender-Bending

Margaret Atwood, *Wilderness Tips* and *Good Bones*: Myths Revisited, Value Added

Both Margaret Atwood and Susan Swan could be perceived, in the light of the proliferation of writings from diverse ethnic minorities, as representative of a White, Anglo-Saxon, literary current. Swan's, and Atwood's later work in particular, engage with the world on the level of irony and parody, concentrating on subverting the social and rhetorical forms which categorize and mould our perceptions. Their writings both come out of a Western, urban, feminist consciousness informed by the emancipatory movements of the 1960s and the ensuing scepticism about relations between the sexes. Such scepticism evolves from an awareness that ideology and language are accomplices in all social power relations.

The subversive thrust of rhetorical strategies such as irony have been heavily debated within the context of postcolonial cultures, and the Canadian one in particular, since, as Gail McGregor observes: "the single adjective most applied to Canadian literature by critics is probably 'ironic'" (McGregor cited in Hutcheon 1991, 4). Linda Hutcheon also maintains that: "[t]here seems little in Canada that is not (or has not been) inherently doubled and therefore at least structurally ripe for ironizing" (Hutcheon 1991, 15), and she has extensively explored the cultural, social and historical forms of such ambivalence. But a fundamental ambivalence, which, as I have attempted to demonstrate, informs the Canadian cultural imaginary in many and diverse ways, does not necessarily take the seemingly ideologically detached forms of Atwood's and Swan's rhetorical play. One could therefore advance tentatively that the perceptions and strategies deployed in both their fictions are not so much to be classified in a general category of "English-speaking fiction" as in that of "Anglo-Saxon, English-speaking fiction" with its exacerbated consciousness of the duplicity involved in particular historical ties to

Britain and to that other Anglo-Saxon power south of the border, the Unitied States. This problematical (because duplicitous) stance not only thematically informs their work, but is also centered in the type of rhetorical hesitation and world-view that irony promotes. These texts thus differ radically from the type of genre scrambling in *The Prowler* for example, where the focus is on cultural difference but through a complex exploration of the hybrid nature of origins themselves. For although heterogeneity defines all the writings in this volume, it takes as its starting point extremely diverse engagements with language(s) and culture(s), and different relationships to subjecthood and history emerge from those engagements.

As the most internationally acclaimed of Canadian writers to have left her mark on the Canadian literary consciousness, Margaret Atwood has worked on defining what it is to be Canadian and a woman since the 1970's. The media have, over the years, done much to produce an icon of successful "Canadianness-in-the-feminine", a representation which other writers have on occasion taken her to task for, as one promoting as universal a singular perspective on Canadian reality, and thus shunning diverse agendas and issues which make up the fabric of the Canadian community. Itwaru has stated, in relation to *Survival*, (Atwood's critical appraisal of the dominant themes and underlying cultural consciousness in Canadian literature): "In *Survival* Atwood attempts to depict a particular mode of consciousness – the victimized, the terrified, people obsessed with gloom ... Arising out of this Atwoodian invention is her search for Canada, one which would seem based on the Enlightenment rationalist concept of the supposed importance of a balance of thought informed out of a centralizing and unifying symbol". (Itwaru 1990, 24).

Atwood has nonetheless become an extremely powerful spokeswoman for social change over the years, and since her novel *Surfacing*, her work has consistently treated both the political "uses and abuses of power" and those which reveal the "misogynistic practices of masculinist culture" (Bouson 1993, 10). She has increasingly, and ironically, investigated what it means to be a woman and a Canadian next to a powerful North American neighbour, and, if her investigations are necessarily partial, because ultimately positional, they are no less pertinent in their challenges to political hegemonies and gender inequalities. Female subjectivity and its inherent ambivalence have indeed been a constant focus in Atwood's work and have been given much critical attention (of which a full-length study by Sonia Mycak) (1996).

If Atwood is best known, and much praised for her novels which cover a wide span of genres, from female quest narrative to dystopia, gothic romance to historiography, her short fiction has attracted less attention. The stories such as those in *Wilderness Tips* and the more difficult to classify pieces in *Good Bones*, with its mixture of several genres, to my mind, not only reveal the topoï which run through her work as a whole and have come to be identified as the Atwood "signature", but exemplify the way Atwood uses genres "not as categories, but as rhetorical strategies or social institutions" (Cooke cited in Howells 2000, 140). She thus works at undermining those "conventions that are presumed to be literary 'universals, ' but can in fact be shown to embody the values of a very particular group of people – of a certain class, race, gender, and sexual orientation" (Hutcheon cited in Howells 2000, 140). What such short fictions foreground is Atwood's retreat from her initial stance of consciousness-raising in *Surfacing* with its polarized representations of power structures, and her move towards a challenging of *discursive* mediums seen as not only reflecting, but inflecting such power structures. As Lorraine York points out, "in all of her work to date, Atwood has undertaken a critique of iconization, that powerful aesthetic and emotional desire to reify" (York 1995, 231-2).

Challenging fixed assumptions on Canada, on social values, and on women has indeed characterized her work from the start. But I would agree with York that in her later works the value of iconoclasm itself is tested as well as the implication of the perceiver's positioning in the act of constructing the icon it challenges. Those fixed representations of cultural power to be dismantled thus become themselves unstable constructs. This, of course, is not to say that victims of political or racial prejudice have in some way "constructed" that prejudice of which they are victims, but that dominant discourses that shut out are not independent constructs which can simply be dismantled, but, on the contrary, rely intimately on the differences they suppress in order to be dominant. Atwood's work has increasingly been informed by the realization that such oppositions are therefore not part of a social, political power standing outside the self, but underpin language and subjectivity, and that, therefore, criticising an unequal power structure does not do away with the process of creating oppositional power structures. This focussing on the process through which values are embedded within representations but equally constructed through representation – Atwood's "political aesthetic" (238) – could be seen as a political disengagement, a playing of increasingly sophisticated and self-conscious language games. One could also argue, however, that such scepticism (and not necessarily cynicism), with regards to cultural sign systems which the multiple slippages of meaning that such an aesthetics deploys, allows for new cognitive spaces to be opened up, and raises questions on both Canadian self-representations and our expectations as readers. Such an aesthetics reveals the ambivalent relationship between social, prescriptive (and not unpleasurable) codes of romance and women's representative status, that is: "The difficulty of curing plot of life, and life of certain plots": (Miller cited in Bouson 1993, 6). Bouson explores the fundamental link between English-speaking Canadian literature and the love/marriage plot. I am, however, once again tempted to substitute "Anglo-Saxon" for "English-speaking" since Atwood's sources are obviously British Gothic or the Victorian novel whereas Hiromi Goto or Aritha van Herk, even though English-speaking Canadian – in the sense that English is the official language they live and work in – come from very different literary and cultural traditions.

Atwood's short fictions, corresponding to what Pierre Tibi has called "the contest between the poetic and the narrative, the spatial and the linear order" (Tibi 1988, 15, translation mine), which is the hallmark of the short story in its concomitant subsuming of plot to form, are ideal vehicles, not only for such a "political aesthetics" but for revealing the tensions and ties linking ethics and aesthetics. The short fiction form has also proved, as Claire Hanson has demonstrated, an ideal vehicle for women writers and submerged' groups in society in that it is capable of registering the gaps and contradictions that signal "a sense of alienation from dominant culture and ideology" (See Hanson 1989, 1-9).

Revisiting History, Reading for Signs

To Victorian England, the search for a Northwest Passage was a romantic adventure that rivaled our late twentieth-century fascination with space exploration. Since the time of Franklin the high Arctic and the search for the passage have become inextricably associated with his name. ... The word "Franklin" has become a sign in a semiotic system of complex, shifting significance (Grace 1995, 149).

In her excellent essay on the story "The Age of Lead" Sherrill Grace thus demonstrates the place John Franklin's nineteenth-century aborted expedition holds in the Canadian cultural imaginary, not only as part of Canadian history, but as one of the "ghosts" doubling contemporary Canadian self-representations. Grace demonstrates that the continuing mystery surrounding the voyage, and its status as a myth, crystalizes questions about the Canadian colonial inheritance and origins. In its doubled aspect, shifting between colonial times and late twentieth-century Canada, and in its challenging the answers science and progress have supposedly provided in our late capitalistic world to disease and pollution, the myth expresses the tensions and anxieties of Canada as a New World culture. One which both seeks to disengage itself from the colonial legacy but nonetheless, partakes in global capitalism's similar logic of mastery and gain. Canada becomes, through Atwood's handling, in this fiction as in others, an unstable frame seeking to accommodate diverse and contingent realities.

The narrative presents several levels, or "framings" of Franklin's voyage seen through the eyes of the female focalizer watching a television screen on which is projected the film "Frozen in Time", a (1987) documentary (which accompanied a book Atwood acknowledges as her source for the story) relating the scientific expedition, the discovery and exhumation of bodies from the expedition. It also featured scientists' explanations and conclusions concerning the mystery of their deaths. However, the intertext of Franklin's adventure in its multiple representations and the "truth" that the scientists' mission announces that, in Grace's words, "the past lies embedded in and fully accessible to the present; that discoveries ... confirm continuities, validate identities and activities" (161), becomes, through Atwood's shifting of frames and blurring of boundaries, a narrative about historical meanings and forms of truth themselves. She thus challenges our assumptions about our scientific production of continuity and knowledge. By interweaving the narrative of Franklin and the lead-poisoning that apparently caused the deaths, with a contemporary one of the narrator's friend Vincent, who died from a mysterious disease, apparently "something [he] ate" (Atwood 1992a, 173), the story creates an interface between past and present; one which problematizes the historical "evidence", "resolution" and "proof" of the documentary intertext of scientific discovery. The story thus indirectly points to modernity's claim to mastery and knowledge as relying on the same arrogant and ill-adapted claims to complete knowledge and solutions as the imperialistic Franklin expedition, and posits, in the image of an urban wasteland at the end, "a city under bombardment" (175), that a similar desastrous result has ensued. Notions of scientific deduction, along with others like "exploration" "discovery" and "recovery": terms belonging to the categories of law, empirical reasoning and territorial appropriation (in short the language and practice of imperialistic domination, but also of contemporary Western society in general), are subjected to a process of conceptual revision. For their primary references, conferred by the "real" events of history, and also the scientifically "legitimate" ones revealed by the documentary, which together provide the crucial intertext of the story, undergo a generic scrambling as codes of romance, gothic and folktale confer differential aspects on them. If, as Todorov has suggested, "[g]enres, like any other institution, reveal the constitutive traits of the society to which they belong", Atwood's incongruous mixing of the description of an exhumed nineteenth-century sailor preserved in ice and "maraschino cherries", his "beige colour, like a gravy stain on linen", his eyeballs "the light brown of milky tea (159-60)"; her dissolving the limits between documentary, scientific "evidence", and banal objects of consumption, all make a statement about the instability of generic categories and, by inference, about the constructedness of value itself.

Likewise, the polyphony provided by a system of echoes linking diverse narrative threads and meanings within the semantic range of a common signifier undermines the stable focus on content provided by the "real" historical facts, in favour of an aesthetics where signs proliferate. The trail of the lost crew "heading south" becomes that of "fairy tales, of bread crumbs or seeds or white stones" (161); the narrator's musings on the fate of the expedition, becomes an inner monologue on the concept of "exploration" itself: "to get onto a boat and just go somewhere, somewhere, mapless, off into the unknown. To launch yourself into fright; to find things out. ... it was like having sex in high school, in those days before the Pill, even if you took precautions" (162). Colonial missions thus become, through metonymic slippage, a comment on social values of a given time. The narrator herself leaves a trail of signifiers linking disparate domains. One is *"consequences"* and we understand that the narrator, "a war baby" (163), was one in her mother's work-worn life. There are also references to the effects of the mysterious expedition, and to the sexual promiscuity of the 60s: "they wanted a life without consequences" (167), as well as references to the results of contemporary society's disregard for the environment: the "toxic dumps, radioactive waste" (172). Atwood thus deploys the unresolved aspect of the expedition as a cultural sign attaching the past to the present through an autopsy of behaviour and values, a autopsy which only serves to pose further questions and produces more opaque signs as a trail for us to follow.

In its questioning of Canadian self-representations, and in its use of generic transgressions "Death by Landscape" shares some of the characteristics of "The Age of Lead" The story produces a supplementary discourse which, like that of the Franklin myth, crystalizes cultural anxieties and contradictions. But "Death by Landscape" not only gives us "a revisionist reading of ... wilderness discourse with its male proprietory ethic" (Howells 1995, 63), but also explicitly stages this discourse within the focus of "a decentred female subject incessantly scarching for her absent other" (64). Thus the narrative, which tells the story of a girl's disappearance at summer camp, defines its concern with the national psyche as a specific concern with the women's place within those national self-representations. The traumatic childhood experience of the (now mature) narrator who witnessed her friend's disappearance, and subsequently collects landscape paintings representing the same wilderness site by Canada's most famous group of artists, thus also, as Howells points out, "ironizes the Group's representation of wilderness, its pieties of place, and its exclusion of the Native inhabitants" (62). This narrative, like "The Age of Lead" gives us trails, traces, speculations and loss, and like many of Atwood's stories, shifts back and forth across boundaries of time. But here the aesthetics of an artistic movement is both questioned and deployed as a strategy in the deconstruction of the value system it upheld. For the empty, "pure" virgin territory of the Group of Seven's representations, which curiously reminds us of a European sublime acsthctics despite its deliberate ideological and thematic departure from European models, here provides the crucial historical intertext; an intertext which, like the Franklin expedition, serves to leave a trail to those signifying absences and complicities informing the Canadian cultural imaginary. The "first real shout ... like a footprint trampled by other footprints" (Atwood 1992, 123) signalling the moment of Lucy's disappearance, the paintings themselves with "no people in them or even animals" yet with "something, or someone, looking back out" (110), the "receding maze, in which you can become lost", and where nonetheless Lucy is "there, in behind the pink stone island" (128-9), give us the effect of an uncanny double, of a split self that is the primary (and heavily investigated) focus of all Atwood's fiction. "Death by Landscape" in its emphasis on the reading of opaque signs, ones which leave traces and trails but which, paradoxically designate ellipse and absence, comes to us interwoven with another set of clearly encoded signs: the artistic aesthetics of an ideologically and historically identifiable period and place. We could say therefore, that while the play on expressive codes allows the stories to question a particular Canadian aesthetics and its nationalist ethos, it also questions the very process of sign production in its aesthetic, historical and social dimensions. The anxiety about points of reference, about the difficulty of "framing" reality, or, as the double Lois/Lucy dramatizes, of fixing the female subject within a stable discursive positioning, indeed serves to problematize the entire notion of subjectivity.

The Feminine Mystique

> For woman is traditionally use-value for man, exchange-value among men. ... How can this object of transaction assert a right to pleasure without extricating itself from the established commercial system? ... How can raw materials possess of themselves without provoking in the consumer fear of the disappearance of his nourishing soil? (Irigaray 1981, 105).

Several of the prose-poems of *Good Bones* could be an imaginative rendering of Luce Irigaray's theoretical formulation of "Woman" as "Other" in the symbolic and political economy. The short pieces comprising the collection, a heterogeneous mixture of genres, are, I would agree, a deployment of "the useful form of the prose poem for [Atwood's] deepest, most biting expression" (Wagner-Martin 1995, 84). For the playful content of these reworkings of folk tales, parables and other popular forms does not diminish their satirical and ironical reach. Atwood is here, as in her longer works, a cultural theorist taking the temperature of contemporary society, but the condensed form of these works underlines the clichés and stereotypes informing our perceptions. "Unpopular Gals" "Let us Now Praise Stupid Women" and "The Female Body" in particular, site "Woman" as object and as construct. The revisionist fairy-tale with the wicked witch as central focus of "Unpopular Gals" thus harbours the narrative kernels of a whole range of cultural narratives. The opposition bad/good girl and the discriminatory operations producing such categories are taken apart in this remake of "Cinderella", but it also connotes a whole range of other less fictional and less playful narratives: seventeenth century witch-hunts for example, or the abrupt and complete silencing of women in Afghanistan; all those instances of cultural anxiety projected onto and contained within the female seen both as desirable and dangerous "Other". But Atwood does not here merely substitute terms. The play and the irony come from the carving out of a gap between encoded forms (like the "Cinderella" one), and the "natural" relation of tales to the world they explore. Atwood denaturalizes this relation by showing the arbitrary positioning of "good" and "bad" according to socially and historically-determined factors, and the way the fear or fantasies that myths or tales generate reflect cultural anxieties and moral imperatives. In the witch's ironically posing the question: "Cooking and eating children ... What a fantasy, and even if I did eat just a few, whose fault was it? Those children were left in the forest by their parents" (Atwood 1992b, 27), Atwood re-places the good/bad structural opposition of the tale in its cultural and literary context, as part of a Western, masculinist mythology.

As the closing lines state: "No Devil, no Fall, no Redemption ... I'm the plot, babe" (30), underlining how "woman" and "witch" could easily be a matching pair in a gendered, and ultimately discursive cultural economy. Similarly, "Let Us Now Praise Stupid Women" reaches further than the anecdotal tone of the piece. The complex intertextual strategies at work, which, as Patricia Merivale has pointed out, take us, in the way of a parody, through the Bible, T.S. Eliot, and Baudelaire as well as Atwood's own work, not only break literary and genre hierarchies but open up the stereotype of the "dumb blond" to expose its cultural underpinnings (See Merivale 1995, 253-70). Yet the opposition between the boringly predictable Wise Virgins of the bible, "their lamps trimmed and filled with oil" (Atwood 1992b, 33), and Eve, one version of the "Eternal Stupid Woman" (34), who "ends up eating the free sample of the apple from the Tree of Knowledge: thus giving birth to Theology" (34) is in fact no simple opposition. For, whereas the masculinist construction of the "dumb blond", the "Wise/not Wise" virgins, or the Creation narrative all suggest the cultural process implicit in such stereotypes, the status of "dumb blond" is not discredited as such. It is in fact difficult to ascertain the direction of the ironical focus – towards men in their need for, and belief in, the naive subterfuges of "dumb blonds", towards the blonds themselves for playing "dumb", towards us the readers for enjoying and identifying so readily with those tabloid or literary heroines, (Atwood's own among them). Just as the processes of myth-making and story-telling themselves are brought to the fore, the unstable focus thus puts the reader up against his/her need to contain and frame, and reveals the way knowledges – "Theology", "Literature" – spring from the same narrative matrix as the popular culture they seek to transcend. As Lorraine York states, Atwood's unstable focus in her later work can be seen as "a profound skepticism about the efficacy of iconoclasm" (York 1995, 239). In fact this prose-poem illustrates – and such is its force to my mind – the rhetorical function of the icon itself, the "dumb blond", as "a paradoxically iconoclastic force", resisting "all attempts to circumscribe its power" (239). Much in the way that "Marilyn Monroe" the icon, can be seen as an uncloseable, and ultimately discursive construct, so the "dumb blond" sited in Atwood's fiction is enmeshed in contradictory identifications which elude any easy framing or deconstruction.

"The Female Body likewise offers a panoply of cultural stereotypes of women to be dismantled: as barbie-doll, as muse, as consumer product, as gothic damsel in distress. Atwood here plays with the female body as the object of conceptual investigation and scientific control: "made of transparent plastic", the "Circulatory System is red, for the heart and arteries, purple for the veins" (Atwood 1992b, 41). In this fiction the female body as a "natural resource" (44), as "a vision of wholeness, ripeness, like a giant melon" (46) glances sideways at Atwood's *The Handmaid's Tale* and the policed female bodies the novel thematizes. In doing so, the poem's female body as abstract concept and cultural construction is shadowed by the Atwood intertext, her "signature" a "bodily" trace troubling the focus, throwing into question which body – material, authorial, textual – is being cited and sited. The female body as the object of scrutiny, of social and scientific control is thus supplemented, and destabilized by Atwood's self-ironizing focus.

Trash or Truth?

If Atwood focusses on gender stereotyping, she also specifically reworks those literary genres and codes which play into social assumptions on women and value. The story "True Trash" as the oxymoron in the title announces, problematizes notions of "high" and "low" culture. The narrative is governed by the stereotypical codes of the romance genre; the frame narrative of sexual initiation and class distinctions at a boys summer camp is infiltrated with the formulaic aspects of the genre to the extent that boundaries between the waitresses' "True Romance" magazines and the happenings at the camp break down. For the narrative is littered with references not only to "trashy" romance magazines but to Austinesque romance plots and 60s pop culture, to which the names "Ronette" and "Darce" testify. The characters as a whole do seem to function as slippery signs, foregrounding Atwood's focus on, and problematizing of, aesthetic forms and literary genres: "There are nine waitresses. There are always nine. Only the names and faces change" (Atwood 1992a, 16). Just as the Victorian plot linked "property" and "propriety", so the consumer bias to sexual relations, in particular regarding women's status is underlined here. For, if "choosing the right man and not making a terrible mistake" motivates the romance plot and governs the fine line between social, moral legitimacy and its opposite (or "truth" and "trash"), Atwood plays around the complicity that exists between capitalism and morals: how self-serving economic practices come to be naturalized through their links to bourgeois values. Donny, for instance, the rich young boy whose brief liaison with Ronette, the "trash" of the piece, reflects on, and is troubled by those values he has learned which equate sexual promiscuity with negative market forces, the control of production and profit with that of filiation and continuity. "Cheap" in this context takes on a complex meaning: a liaison with a working-class female threatens that paternal order of "propriety" as lawful family continuity, which is intricately linked to the capitalistic logic of "property". However, and here Atwood turns things around and renders such a logic problematical, "[m]ost of the things in his life are expensive, and not very interesting" (10), whereas Ronette's "cheap" act which provides his sexual initiation holds great personal value for him. The market logic of "interest" which guides sexual "interest" thus breaks down under the pressure of his personal interest. For, despite his mother's warnings about girls with "pierced ears" (16), and the fact that he "knows he's supposed to feel [consumer] lust for her", "this is not what he feels" (10). If the sustained emphasis on codes and processes of encoding, through the theme of "woman as object" and the romance scenario, on one level target the value systems that underpin our consumer cultures, they also target the "dissociation between popular objects of consumption and their consumers" (Irvine 2000, 212-3). As such, the story reveals the way we are all called upon to participate in the circulation of goods and culture, a circulation which in turn relies, for its success, on "the production of needs and consumers" (Bourdieu cited in Irvine 2000, 211).

The reconnecting of subjective perceptions to values and contemporary culture is operated through the emphasizing of how we are not above or beyond the consumer codes which produce such clichés, but how our subjectivity is engaged within that same circuit. This constitutes the political thrust of such a playing with form which "True Trash" through its slippery surfaces, reveals. The overblown images such as "ruminating mouths glistening and deep red like mushed-up raspberries" (10) characterizing the "town girls" which Donny is forbidden to consort with, are indistinguishable from those of the "True Romance" magazine. Darce whose "teeth are the whitest, … hair the blondest, his grin the sexiest" (20) is of the same descriptive material as the magazine hero. As the hierarchy between levels of narrative collapses, our way of discriminating between cultural categories of "high" and "low" is questioned. But our apparent dissociation from those representative forms of culture is equally brought to the fore: the way we are "produced", so to speak, as subjects through that same culture. The "oval hills of pink granite" (23) and the "soft ripe juicy

moon" (24), render a "way of seeing the world as an aesthetic phe-
nomenon", one that complies with Susan Sontag's definition of Camp
culture. She speaks of: "a new, more complex relation to the 'seri-
ous'", the collapsing of the "distinction between the unique object and
the mass-produced object" (Sontag 1961, 288-9). The type of stereotypical representations and clichés so characteristic of Atwood's
strategies, and which are central to her short works, are then not to be
seen as a relinquishing of emotional, ethical commitment to her subject matter but rather the opposite. For such clichés, far from expressing an accrued distance between subject and world seek to renew
links, but on the very terms of the reproductive, disconnected culture
we live in. The reproductive quality of clichés themselves, in a social
context where "repetition appears as the welcome instrument of nor-
malising discourses" (Amossy and Rosen 1982, 7, translation mine),
serves not only to underline the implication of language in ideology
but, in Atwood's poetics, seeks new modes of reconnection between
subject and world. When the "nausea of the replica" (Sontag 1961,
289) of our cultures is overcome precisely through the reinstating of
culturally "used" forms, it designates language itself as implicated in
the process of consumerism which takes in both readers and texts.

   The romance plots which Atwood's fiction thus "uses and abuses",
reducing them in her short works to their most condensed formulas,
could be seen as constructing a "feminist 'reading position'" which
has been theorized as: "'the position assumed by a reader from which
the text seems to be coherent and intelligible' – by revealing 'the contradictions and injustices within the dominant gender discourse' and
making visible 'the strategies by which that discourse is naturalized".
(Cranny-Francis cited in Bouson 1993, 8). Such a position, by stressing those processes of emplotment whereby ideology, romance and
narrative interweave and cohere, is not the only valid one, nor does it
purport to be. As the term "position" implies, and as Atwood herself
makes clear, she gives voice to perceptions emerging from her own
particular inscription in a Canadian social and cultural history. One
random quote from Atwood's now well-documented refusal to be
pigeon-holed as striving to speak for any kind of ideological unitary
truth renders: "A lot of the things that one observes as a novelist
looking at life indicated that women are not being treated equally. But
that comes from observation. It doesn't come from ideology. ... none
of the writers that I know, including ones who are regularly defined as
feminists, would say that they are embodying somebody's party line"
(see Atwood 1992c, 140-1).

Susan Swan, *The Wives of Bath*: the Female Body in Question

I sat down in the long grass near the ravine fence. It was just the spot Virginia
Woolf would have picked if she'd gone to Bath Ladies College (Swan 1994, 65).

The Wives of Bath has much in common with Atwood's *Lady Oracle*: the gothic subtext and Victorian intertexts, the themes of masquerade and the double which Swan, like Atwood, deploys in order to
problematize female identity, or the focus on alternative literary and
social encodings in which the narrator is actively engaged. The narrator is a writer of historical romance novels in *Lady Oracle*, while, in
Swan's novel, she is a schoolgirl correspondent and worshiper of John
Kennedy. Both novels are concerned with code-making and code-
breaking, with the strategies of irony which drive a wedge between
language and meaning and which question a Canadian national and
literary colonial inheritance from a feminist perspective. Yet as Diana
Brydon points out, all feminist agendas are not identical, they are articulated across private and public discursive boundaries that are more
or less complex. If Atwood examines, as does Swan, "the onerous
cultural work that goes into the construction of the Canadian woman",
Native women's writing, like Black or Asian Canadian writing, "also
interrogate[s] constructions of racial purity and miscegenation, greatly
complicating our understanding of feminisms and nationalisms" (Brydon 1994, 35).

Swan, like Atwood, plays upon the slipperiness of language codes
themselves, their stable centres and mobile edges, in order to challenge the processes by which reality is "naturalized". Similarly, in
Swan's novel, the female body crystalizes a preoccupation with the
constructedness of gender in patriarchal society, and with female
subjecthood as the negative term in a gender binary which erases difference in the interests of "women's socially produced and policed
gender roles" (see Brydon 1994, 23-45). In *The Wives of Bath* the
whole problem of gender as a stable category is examined through the
very process of challenging genre categories. These two perspectives
of the novel open up a further questioning of Canada's complicity and
resistance in relation to other ideological and historical limits. The
cross-dressing of the narrative could be seen as crystalizing the anxiety that has characterized the colonial encounter in so far as, according to Brydon, it signals other cultural "crossings" and ambivalences.
Cross-dressing thus becomes the narrative symptom of a contested
and conflictual meaning. In the narrative it serves to register both national and transnational affiliations and ambivalences, just as it signals, by inference, the crisis of Canadian identity written into Anglo-

centered imperialist assumptions of superiority over the (French-speaking, First Nations) "Other": a hegemony which was (and some critics would argue still is) part and parcel of the Canadian nation-building enterprise.

Code-Making, Code-Breaking

The Wives of Bath, as the intertextual resonance of the title implies, plays along the limits of genre categories. Just as it points us to Chaucer, so the novel also ironizes the Victorian orphan narrative: the central character Mouse Bradford with her hump she calls "Alice", named "after [Mouse's] real mother ... from the German name *Adelaide*, meaning 'of noble birth'", lands up in a mock-Victorian turreted institution, reminiscent of *Jane Eyre*. Moreover, references to codes of royalty and Victorian values abound: "Bath Ladies College" is modelled after a Norman castle, originally designed "to entertain Queen Victoria" (Swan 1994, 13), there are satirical glances at quirks and customs of the British monarchy, (for example, a corgi here accompagnies a dwarf), and also puns on names; ("Victoria Quinn"/"Queen Victoria"). If codes provide a metafictional exercise in deciphering intertexts and genres in the narrative, they also represent the institutional practices at the mock British boarding-school, where codes of conduct have to be learnt and revised: "Mary Beatrice, you didn't get her cue. When she asks you if you'd like a banana, you're supposed to say 'No thank you'"(57). Furthermore, when Paulie (alias Lewis), the cross-dressing school-girl, initiates Mouse into the art of being a boy, the latter has another series of codes to internalize. The narrative thus thematizes the process of genre construction in its literary, but also psycho-analytical and social policing aspects; the dwarf's castration by Paulie/Lewis is a playing out of the Freudian oedipal narrative, ironizing Freud's founding principles of penis envy and castration anxiety. His murder leads to a courtcase scene, focussing further on the encoded nature of official discourses. The concentration on the functions of dissection, analysis and knowledge production in the narrative creates interfaces between the domains of science, language and the law; Mouse's father is the surgeon Morley and his talent with a scalpel, a scalpel that could "plunge into the realm of malformed bodies and hunt down the symptoms" (190), is compared to Hemingway's insensitive literary "treatment" when, in his stories, he "cut up pregnant Indian ladies and didn't care how loudly they screamed" (190). Morley's surgical skills on prostrate subjects connects with the court's formal procedure of display and dissection of the evidence, since the surgeon's scalpel, wielded for the amateur operation on the dwarf, has now become a courtroom exhibit. The doctor's dexterity with a surgical instrument is furthermore compared to the rhetorician's, and his lack of skill with "parallel sentence structure" countered by the "jumbled words" which make his patients' "heart rates lower" (53).

Domains of medical and rational science interlock and provide a concerted interrogation on the nature of knowledge-production itself, their reliance on the discrimination, the discipline, and the regulation of causes and effects, whether the evidence of a crime or that of sick, thus "unruly" bodies. This points to how the narrative is engaged in examining how subjects are defined and modelled through the "genres" or structures which represent them, how, in Foucault's words, "the subjects regulated by such structures are ... formed, defined, and reproduced in accordance with the requirements of those structures (Foucault cited in Butler 1990a, 2). But precisely where *The Wives of Bath* most concentrates on, and conflates those knowledges which constitute both literary genres and subjectivity, it also posits other types of subjectivity which, as we shall see, metaphorically "disfigure" and "re-figure" the cultural text.

Unruly Subjects

Writing on the figure of the female giant in Swan's *The Biggest Modern Woman in the World* Teresa Heffernan has stated: "[t]here is no [literary, mythological] context for a female giant" (Heffernan 1992, 25). Thus Swan invents a new context for an outrageous female subjectivity, one that "disfigures" the landscape of "normal" gender expectations. She sheds light on the way that "inferior" subjects are constructed through society's reliance on a visual economy, one by which "freaks" are judged, and marginalized as subjects through their "different" bodies. Yet such prejudice serves to underline that if bodies are "read" and attributed a superior or inferior consciousness as an effect of this reading, the "norm" is itself a construct. Swan's freak culture reworks, by inference, the type of fetishistic ambivalence motivating racial and sexual prejudice, the "fantasy of origin and identity" (Bhabha 1994, 67) which for Bhabha is a staging of castration anxiety as both a fixation and disavowal of difference. Such a fantasy of wholeness, which the threat of castration and sexual difference threatens, is "predicated as much on mastery and pleasure as it is on anxiety and defence" (75). The play of blurred sexualities and blurred body boundaries in Swan's novels thus invokes a challenge to, and staging of, the set of contradictory symbolic forces governing subjec-thood, it also envisages the possibility of other types of imaginary identification, of other modes of subjecthood.

The multiple references to distorted, excessive or unusual anato-mies which are central to *The Wives of Bath* – Mouse's hump, Mor-ley's height and impressive genitals, the dwarf, not to mention the repeated allusions to uncommon size or shape: "toy-sized" bodies, cheeks "abnormally swollen", the "rows of breasts bulging out of their blouses-some pairs large and jolly as pumpkins; others, in the stiff, pointed cups of their bras, narrow and sharp" (Swan 1993, 27, 29, 63), render interpretations of "normal" and "deviant" structuring premises of the narrative. For, the world of the college, despite its excessive reliance on codes of conduct and its policing of boundaries is, as Mouse's stepmother points out, a place where "[t]hey like misfits" (17). The focussing on all sorts of transgressions and deviations, from the signifying distorsion of the characters' names-as-puns, to the ho-mosexual bond of the head-teacher, through to the corporeal "distor-sions" deployed as a "natural" part of the institutional world of the college, provides a further distancing, and ironizing of, settled notions of categories themselves. Like the theme of cross-dressing which will be examined in greater detail, the structuring excesses and blurrings set up a field of signs which point to the interdependency and the contamination existing between apparently separate domains of knowledge.

As Heffernan observes, in relation to strategies employed in *The Biggest Modern Woman in the World*, Bakhtin's reading of Rabelais cites (and sites) carnivalesque disruption within the social and politi-cal sphere as a contamination of high culture by the "grotesque" body of the populace. *The Wives of Bath* engages in a similar project of contamination, circulating the multiple figures of excess as a system of signs setting up differences and foregrounding the "co-mingling and impurity of communities" (Heffernan 1992, 33). The ultimately performative aspect of the narrative, as it stages the processes by which subjective spaces and categories are constructed and re-evaluated, amounts to a textual reconfiguring of the logic of identity-construction itself, and of its ambivalent resistances and desires as factors in that construction.

The ultimately mobile, unstable nature of genres, whether that of social, institutional values, or of gender as embodied value, is made clear in the narrative's attention not only to body boundaries but to spatial limits, which are anxiously delineated: the "wire mesh of the ravine fence" which encircles the school and imprisons the schoolgirl

Paulie is "swallowed up" in a fog; it is also the site of mistaken identities: "[w]e were deep into the ravine now, among fallen logs and
ferns ... people in the city mistake for a real forest"; limits are also
encoded as the heterogeneous space of "[s]tyrofoam and dead leaves
... a swampy patch ... by the funny small sandy shore" (Swan 1993,
84, 5, 122).

The permeable and mutating aspect of boundaries, the dilating and
retracting of distances in relation to such limits would comply, in poetic terms, to what the anthropologist Henrietta L. Moore theorizes as:
"gendered spaces ... less as a geography imposed by patriarchal
structures, and more as a 'series of homologies between the spatial,
symbolic and social orders'" (Moore cited in Blunt and Rose, 1994,
3).

If the distinction between public (masculine assertive) and private
(feminine graceful) space was part and parcel of a European "cultural
project of an emerging middle class" from the "early nineteenth century onward" (Davidoff and Hall cited in Blunt and Rose 1994, 3),
thus conflating gender issues with those of class, Bath Ladies College
is in itself a colonial re-presentation of such a Victorian gendered
space in a contemporary context, over-written with the power relations that the production of compulsory femininity implies. It playfully highlights, in all the strands of "learning to be a lady" and the
inverse ones of "learning to be a boy" that criss-cross and collide in
the narrative, the conflicted aspect and non-separation between the
apparently distinct areas of imperialism and gender. One could add,
given the narrative's focus on the reproduction of British colonial
values and practices in a Canadian context, that such anxieties of limits and thresholds registered in the lights of Toronto seen flickering
beyond the limit of the ravine, in its simultaneous imprisoning/ mutating aspect, serves to rhetorically interrogate the ambivalences and
erasures at the core of the settling enterprise.

In her article on "cross-cultural cross-dressing" Brydon reminds us
of the "many possible meanings of *cross* and *double-cross* to suggest
[its] slipperiness, inherent hybridity, and multivalent possibilities in an
invader-settler colony such as Canada" (Brydon 1994, 25). Such slipperiness is at work in *The Wives of Bath*'s neo-colonial boarding-
school regime, where one of the several "crossings" is that of the
school itself in a merger with a boy's school, one where "most of [the
teachers] were British ... in the English tradition of a classical education" (Swan 1993, 111). Furthermore, the codes at work in the production of "ladies" after a British model are themselves compromised;
they are a prey to slippage from the double vision of "Brit-

ish/Canadian", which itself is framed within a third perspective: that of Mouse's infatuation, and correspondance with President Kennedy. This provides a further generic disruption as Swan gives us an ironic re-appraisal of the *Bildungsroman* since Mouse comes to awareness through a fantasied relation with the President, himself largely a product of twentieth-century media iconizing technology. Underlining the polaroid aspect of Kennedy, (who initiated the practice of careful image-production of political figures by the media), Mouse asserts: "You always look brand-new, Mr Kennedy. Whether you are clapping at Caroline doing a handstand in your office or smiling down at her" (48, 9). Mouse's fixation on Kennedy also anchors the narrative in an additional cultural perspective by providing a view-point that is exterior to the world of the school and thus supplements the binary equation Canada/Britain. The American "absent presence" thus allows for the narrative configuring of another opposition: that of Canada as a "gentle giant" in the guise of Morley the expert, but under-rated and absent-minded surgeon, set against the glossy image of Kennedy. The narrative's underscoring of the familiar traits of ideological machinery at work – Kennedy as devoted family-man, war-hero, man-of-the-people – allows for the further problematization of notions of affiliation and difference, of technologies of production, whether those of cultural myths, of political alliances or those of fiction. Furthermore, Mouse's letter-writing to Kennedy introduces the notion of "the third" element, which the overdetermined focus on gender-crossing in the narrative extends even further. The "third" is taken here in the sense that Marjorie Garber explores, one which involves and enables a move "from a structure of complementarity or symmetry to a contextualisation" (Garber 1992, 12). The other (American) anglophone influence as the "third" in the narrative thus constitutes an interruption and re-contextualisation of the enclosed world represented by Bath College, a shift which provides a mobile perspective on notions of independence and affiliation themselves, in the context of a multiaffiliated country such as Canada. For, as Garber says further – and that I will examine in relation to cross-dressing – "the third is not a term but a mode of articulation, a way of describing a space of possibility" (11).

Performing Gender

Gender is a performance with clearly punitive consequences. Discrete genders are part of what 'humanizes' individuals within contemporary culture; indeed, those who fail to do their gender right are regularly punished (Butler cited in Gabriel 1994, 237).

The Wives of Bath illustrates both the struggle to "do one's gender right" and the consequences for failure. Whereas one schoolgirl follows "the nightly ritual" (Swan 1993, 94) for a good complexion and other feminine virtues, Paulie, alias Lewis, devises an eight-point initiation into being a boy. The homosexual relationship between two female teachers finishes in police brutality and renunciation of the headship of the school, while the gardener is castrated in order to provide Paulie with the "gender-dressing" she/he lacks. In these and the other contests in conforming to gender expectations, and culminating in the castration in all its Freudian, dramatic significance, the emphasis is on gender as an effort to "do it right"; a performance within the process of become a subject, "something that is achieved rather than given and that is inherently at risk" (Gabriel 1994, 242).

In situating gender disturbance and control at the centre of the narrative, and in putting cross-dressing at the heart of the narrative's slippages, Swan is questioning the "naturalizing strategy" of sexual and subjective development. But the choice of such gender blurring also feeds into wider issues, those of interrogating the "other ideological work [which] is being accomplished in the anchoring of sexual identities in discrete historical moments" (242). For indeed, when Paulie "becomes" Lewis temporarily she stages the symbolic crisis at the heart of the subject's gender identification by confounding those distinctions which ground identities in a binary symetry which is "concceivcd as stablc, unchallcngcablc, groundcd, and 'known'". (Garber 1992, 13). If cross-dressing renders Paulie's outside masculine while her "essence", her sexuality, is female, it also symbolizes the opposite: that her "real" desire or gender identification is masculine, while her "dressing", the gendered body, is female (Newton cited in Butler 1990a, 137). As Judith Butler adds: *"In imitating gender, drag implicitly reveals the imitative structure of gender itself – as well as its contingency"* (1990a, 137). As she demonstrates at length, cross-dressing is a displacement of the notions of "origin" and "truth" since they bring into play not only the naturalized links between the subject's gendered, social "appearance" and sexual anatomy, but also rely on the permutation of three terms: sexuality, gender, and performed gender. Within the theatre of cross-dressing the distinction between the three and their contingency is brought to the fore: the way heterosexuality naturalizes them as an indissoluble unity. Cross-dressing, in staging the culturally fabricated unity we think of as a "normal" one, thus becomes, not the parody of an original but "the parody ... *of* the very notion of an original" (138),

Paulie's drastic act, where she treats the body literally as exchange-able costume in order to appropriate the anatomical "dressing" she lacks, is the narrative's climax to the process of defamiliarization it puts in play around notions of sexual identity and social representa-tions, around corporeal boundaries and their relation to psychic space, around the rigid distinctions between inner and outer which construct an inner "truth" of the body. As Mary Douglas says: "the body is a model that can stand for any bounded system. Its boundaries can rep-resent any boundaries which are threatened or precarious" (Douglas cited in Butler 1990a, 132). *The Wives of Bath*, in its concentration on such limits, on exposing the fabricated aspect of gender identity, stages the cultural anxiety of permeable boundaries. The political and social signifying aspect of Swan's playing around the site of the body's construction and deconstruction is rendered in the descriptive (and literal) dismemberment which the narrative operates; Mouse spends much time pondering the relative values of possessing a penis which "is not as long proportionately as, say, the genitals of the Hors-eneck clam" (113) when studying her father's copy of *Gray's Anat-omy*, in which the female genitals are described as "a head with wild, wavy hair spreading like flames around its face. And this face had no features except two small open wailing mouths calling out in distress" (207). Disconnected body parts take on the aspect of a challenge not only to identity as a stable category, but to unified, stable categories or systems in general.

As Susan Stewart says, examining the imaginary function of the "grotesque body" in medieval carnival and contemporary culture: "The parading of the grotesque is often the isolation and display of the exaggerated part ... This scattering and redistribution of bodily parts is the antithesis of the body as a functional tool ... The free exchange, substitution, and interpenetration of bodily elements ... is sympto-matic of the exchange of the fair and marketplace which provides its context" (Stewart 1984, 105).

Moreover, the textual defamiliarization at work and its centering on the body as a political site can been linked to what both Brydon and Gabriel say about cross-dressing in relation to Canadian literature. Examining a range of Canadian texts figuring a cross-dresser or a cross-cultural dresser (in the sense of crossing the social/cultural boundaries set out as norms), Brydon underlines the ambivalence of such fictions which "seem to signal the ambivalence at the heart of the imperialist civilizing enterprise in Canada", demonstrating how "closely interwoven the construction of gender and nation have been throughout Canada's literary history." (1994, 40-1). Gabriel stresses the specifically performative aspect of such Canadian cultural and/or dress crossing, giving the example of Timothy Findley's *Not Wanted on the Voyage* whose character Lucy/Lucifer embodies "gender instability, mimesis, cross-dressing, and theatricality", Atwood's Joan Foster of *Lady Oracle* "a Houdini-like escape-artist who cannot really escape her social scripting", or Alice Munro's "feminine body already saturated with language and culture" (1994, 243-4). Paulie, alias Lewis, of *The Wives of Bath* similarly portrays both characteristics of gender-blurring and cultural boundary-blurring as she/he rejects the laws of Bath College's civilising and feminizing mission.

It would appear then, that the excessive, transformative, "crossing" body that Swan's novel stages is both a gendered and a culturally indeterminate site that raises questions on sexual difference and national indeterminancy. The textual refiguring of spaces and boundaries, the emphasis on encodings and decodings, crystalize the anxieties of a culture still coming to terms with its "settler-invader" (Brydon 1994, 25) status, one which articulates "Canadianness ... through crossed constructions of competing narratives of nation and gender" (24). The ironical perspective on those "civilizing" European codes of conduct which Bath College gives us, while emphasizing both their contingency and their centering on the ideologically charged site of the female body, is concerned with the possible scripting of alternative subjectivities. Mouse, like Elaine Risley of Atwood's *Cat's Eye*, is negotiating subject positions, neither able to fit into the stereotypical frame of the neo-Victorian "lady" that the college promotes, nor fully to identify with the masculine positioning of Kennedy, her hero with a similarly afflicted back. Through her being situated within a series of overlapping thresholds, none of the discourses (rather like the orthopaedic supports she is obliged to wear), "fit" exactly. Similarly, the narrative, in its entirety, does not provide closure to the problem of what constitutes "fitting" conduct, or a "fit" female body, or how to "fit" the former to the latter. We are left, as it were, at the cultural and textual crossroads of a narrative which makes category constructing its main focus, and thereby contributes to a questioning of representations of all kinds.

Conclusion

[T]he notion of the 'category crisis, ' I will contend, is not the exception but the ground of culture itself (Garber 1992, 16).

As Swan's novel exemplifies, cross-dressed figures serve as an index of crisis elsewhere, a "displacement from one blurred boundary to another" (16) and the fictions presented in this volume all deal in displacements: in crises of categories through which the constructedness and vulnerability of culture is made evident. At the centre of these problems of definition is the category of gender itself which informs all the writings, usually as a thematic focus but as a textual modality as well. The damaged Caribbean psyche of Brand's stories and novel have as their starting-point and poetic condition, the community body as female, saturated with the oral language of memory and put under erasure as the colonial "Other". The hybridity of such writing matches the polyphony of Goto's textual space which "re-figures" (in the sense of inventing other sets of signs) the cultural landscape, in order to accommodate Japanese/Canadian female picaresque versions of the "house and horse" narratives of the prairie. The role of language itself as the mobile interface between the self and place, its continual production of discriminations and differences, is also relevant to van Herk's narrative of place as textual space. The textual encounter of geography with a diasporic consciousness in Michaels' novel, both trailing and retracing the "fugitive pieces" of memory, once again subsumes subjective experience to the signifying process of displacement and slippage, between disparate systems of knowledge, as if "location", in the sense of a subjective and objective situatedness, could only be thought within the framework of aesthetic forms which challenge the very categories of "inner" and "outer" psychic space on which such distinctions rely. Similarly, for Gunnars and Brossard, challenging those distinct knowledges and oppositions which create cultural differences becomes a creative investigation into how culture itself – social and political, – is an effect of language, of an inherently gendered language whose subjective, bodily premises mark the emergence of sexual difference.

The oppositional categories of "subjective " and "objective" the m-selves thus give way, in these writings, to negotiations between overlapping discursive areas, knowledges, and erasures – poetical/resistance (Brand), symbolic/imaginary identification (Lau), irony/political aesthetic (Atwood) – to suggest only a few of those at work.

Which brings me back to Braidotti's definition of subjectivity, which initially provided a working definition for examining this selection of Canadian women's fiction. If both the material and the symbolic forces at work, implying both enablement and limits, are part of the multiple discourses (and therefore thresholds) which both condition and constitute subjecthood itself, then the conflict between a political agency or "will" governing language, and the post-structuralist dismantling of all fixed identity within language, can be surpassed.

In the same way, concerning narrative, the opposition between theme as content expressing a political/ethical vision, and aesthetic form, proves to be a sterile one in postcolonial literatures. These are literatures where disrupted, fragmented, "postmodern" strategies do not evacuate politics in a vertiginous spiral of language, an "aestheticising of the political" but instead foreground "the political as inevitably contaminating the aesthetic" (Brydon 1991, 192-3). In this context, Linda Hutcheon is cited, and brought to task by Diana Brydon for maintaining that: "post-structuralist/post-modern challenges to the coherent, autonomous subject have to be put on hold in feminist and postcolonial discourses, for both must work first to assert and affirm a denied or alienated subjectivity" (Hutcheon cited in Brydon 1991, 193). In writing where personal and historical discontinuities produce a fundamental heterogeneity, where there is a complex relation to Canadian space as both "lived in" place and value system, seeking out the elusive traces of subjective erasure (Lau), or discovering the more evident thematic and rhetorical markers of displacement (Mayr), are equally valid critical practices to my mind. The criticisms levelled at Lau for example, revealing the expectations that her texts comply with an agenda of "ethnic" realism, (rather ironically, given the "master narratives" postcolonial criticism is engaged in dismantling), set a prescriptive agenda for "politically correct" texts. If political challenge is overtly situated within social and cultural representations, it is also, as we now know, woven into the strategies that language itself uses as both a means of communication and of foreclosure.

Admittedly, any and all readings are necessarily partial, the specificity of postcolonial writing is both its often insistent demand that we participate actively in the construction of meaning (van Herk, Brossard), but also that we question our own sets of values and challenge the comfort of our "situatedness" in society and culture. For such texts confront us with the final inadequacy of any "true" reading of an other, not because this other is inadequate, but because we, as readers, are. Happily so. For it this very resistance to allowing us totalizing readings, denying us the power to assign our own identifications as meaning, which characterizes the texts in this volume. Their interest, in a way, is contrary to mine; they challenge the type of closures I am drawn to make, since interpretation is inevitably the structuring of another subjectivity (mine), across the weave of the subjectivity which both confronts and opens itself to me. Since, if my reading is both inadequate and incomplete, it is nonetheless self-interested. I am drawn into the text(s) in the hope that my act of elucidation will elucidate my own desire for reading, my own will to self-knowledge. If the admission that my own subjective positioning is not outside my act of reading but at the centre of it constitutes in itself a politics, then such a politics of reading, ultimately positional, partial and provisional, is to my mind what legitimizes the field and practice of postcolonial criticism itself.

The placings and displacements of the female subject in Canadian texts, the imaginary retrievals and thresholds which such writings articulate, will, hopefully, find no adequate closure here. The movement from one blurred boundary to another which characterizes the texts studied in this volume, and which concomitantly identifies my own perception of culture, opens up the notion of subjectivity itself. As such, the textual politics and the play(s) of difference constitute both the specificity of these women's writings, and their participation in the more general fictional and critical enterprise of interrogating culture in all its encodings. The complex cross-cultural subjectivity at the core of Canadian nationhood and of its literary production thus also informs a critical reflection on the construction of unified discourses, providing a model of the complex, and ultimately unstable institutional, social and cultural codes we all participate in and are "invented" by.

Works Cited

Adam, Ian and Helen Tiffin, eds. 1991. *Past the Last Post: Theorizing Postcolonialism and Post-Modernism*. New York: Harvester Wheatsheaf.

Adorno, Theodor W. 1973. *Negative Dialectics*. In Cook, 12.

Amossy, Ruth and Elisheva Rosen. 1982. *Les Discours du cliché*. Paris: S.E.D.E.S, C.D.U.

Ashcroft, W.D., Gareth Griffiths and Helen Tiffin. 1989. *The Empire Writes Back: Theory and practice in post-colonial literatures*. London/New York: Routledge.

Ashcroft, W.D. 1989. "Constitutive Graphonomy: A Postcolonial Theory of Literary Writing". In *After Europe: Critical Theory and Postcolonial Writing*, edited by Stephen Slemon and Helen Tiffin, 58-73. Sydney/Mundelstrup: Dangaroo Press.

—. 1994. "EXCESS: Postcolonialism and the verandahs of meaning". In *De-Scribing Empire: Postcolonialism and textuality*, edited by Chris Tiffin and Alan Lawson, 33-44. London/New York: Routledge.

Atwood, Margaret. [1985] 1987. *The Handmaid's Tale*. London: Virago.

—. 1972. *Survival: A Thematic Guide to Canadian Literature*. Toronto: Anansi.

—. [1972] 1979. *Surfacing*. London: Virago.

—. [1991] 1992a. "The Age of Lead" in *Wilderness Tips*. London: Virago.

—. 1992b. *Good Bones*. Toronto: Coach House Press.

—. 1992c. Interview by Jo Brans. "Using What You're Given". In *Margaret Atwood: Conversations*, edited by Earl G. Ingersoll, 140-51. London: Virago.

Barthes, Roland. [1957] 1973. *Mythologies*. St. Albans: Paladin.

—. 1973. *Le Plaisir du texte*. Paris: Seuil.

Bakhtin, Mikhail. [1965] 1984. *Rabelais and his World*. Bloomington: Indiana University Press.

—. [1975] 1981. "Discourse in the Novel". In *The Dialogic Imagination: Four Essays by M. M. Bakhtin*, edited by M. Holquist, 259-423. Austin: University of Texas Press. 1981.

Baudrillard, Jean. [1968] 1988. "The System of Objects". In *Jean Baudrillard; Selected Writings*, edited by Mark Poster, 10-28. Cambridge: Polity Press.

Bauman, Zygmunt. 1991. *Modernity and the Holocaust*. Ithaca/New York: Yale University Press.

Beauregard, Guy. 1999. "The Emergence of 'Asian Canadian Literature': Can Lit's Obscene Supplement?" *Essays on Canadian Writing*, 67 (Spring): 53-75.

Beautell, Eva Darias. 2000. "Writing Back and Beyond: Postcoloniality, Multiculturalism, and Ethnicity in the Canadian Context". In *Tricks with a Glass: Writing Ethnicity in Canada*, edited by Rocío G. Davis and Rosalía Baena, 19-35. Amsterdam-Atlanta: Rodopi.

Benjamen, Walter. 1969. *Illuminations*. In Kamboureli, 2000, 96.

Berton, Pierre. 1992. *Niagara: A History of the Falls*. In Mayr, 13.

Bhabha, Homi K., ed. 1990. "DissemiNation: time, narrative, and the margins of the modern nation". In *Nation and Narration*, 291-322. London/New York: Routledge.

—. 1994. *The Location of Culture*. London: Routledge.

Blanchot, Maurice. [1980] 1986. *The Writing of the Disaster*. In Langer, 69.

Blunt, Alison, and Gillian Rose, eds. 1994. *Writing Women and Space: Colonial and Postcolonial Geographies*. New York/London: The Guilford Press.

Bourdieu, 1984. *Distinction: A Social Critique of the Judgement of Taste*. In Irvine, 211.

Bouson, J. Brooks. 1993. *Brutal Choreographies: Oppositional Strategies and Narrative Design in the Novels of Margaret Atwood*. Amherst: The University of Massachusetts Press.

Braidotti, Rosi. 1994. *Nomadic Subjects: Embodiment and Sexual Difference in Contemporary Feminist Theory*. New York: Columbia University Press.

Brand, Dionne. 1990. Interview by Dagmar Novak. In *Other Solitudes: Canadian Multicultural Fictions*, edited by Linda Hutcheon, 263-77.

—. 1998. Interview by Beverley Daurio. "Writing It". In *The power to Bend Spoons: Interviews with Canadian Novelists*, edited by Beverley Daurio, 31-41. Toronto: The Mercury Press.

—. 1988. *Sans Souci and other Stories*. Stratford, Ontario: Williams-Wallace.

—. [1996] 1997. *In Another Place, Not Here*. London: The Women's Press.

Brock, Sabine. 1996. "A Trace of Body Writing: Morrison's *Beloved*". *G.R.A.A.T.* 14 ("Ethnic Voices II"), 125-30.

Brossard, Nicole. [1985] 1988. *The Aerial Letter*. Toronto: The Women's Press.

—. [1980] 1989. *Surfaces of Sense*. Toronto: Coach House Québec Translations.

—. [1987] 1990. *Mauve Desert*. Toronto: Coach House Press.

—. 1993. Interview by Janice Williamson. "Before I became a feminist, I suppose I was an angel, a poet, a revolutionary…". In Janice Williamson, *Sounding Differences: Conversations with Seventeen Canadian Women Writers*, 59-72. Toronto: University of Toronto Press.

Browning, Christopher R. 1983. "The German Bureaucracy and the Holocaust". In Bauman, 13.

Brydon, Diana. 1991. "The White Inuit Speaks: Contamination as Literary Strategy". In *Past the Last Post: Theorizing Post-Colonialism and Post-Modernism*, edited by Ian Adam and Helen Tiffin, 191-203. New York: Harvester Wheatsheaf.

—. 1994. "'Empire Bloomers': Cross-Dressing's Double Cross". *Essays on Canadian Writing*, 54 (Winter): 23-45.

Butler, Judith. 1990a. *Gender Trouble: Feminism and the Subversion of Identity*. New York/London: Routledge.

—. 1990b. "Performative Acts and Gender Constitution: An Essay in Phenomenology". In Gabriel, 237.

Cameron, Barry. 1987. "Lacan: Implications of Psychoanalysis and Canadian Discourse" in *Future Indicative: Literary Theory and Canadian Literature*, edited by John Moss, 137-51. Ottawa, University of Ottawa Press.

Chow, Rey. 1995. *Primitive Passions. Visuality, Sexuality, Ethnography, and Contemporary Chinese Cinema*. In Kamboureli, 2000, 96.

Cixous, Hélène. [1976] 1981. "The Laugh of the Medusa". In *New French Feminisms: An Anthology*, edited by Elaine Marks and Isabelle de Courtivron, 245-64. Brighton: Harvester.

Chamberlain, Lori. 1992. "Gender and the Metaphorics of Translation". In *Rethinking Translation: Discourse, Subjectivity, Ideology*, edited by Lawrence Venuti, 57-74. London/New York, Routledge.

Coleman, Daniel. 1994. "Gender, Narrative, and Desire in *The Prowler*". *Textual Studies in Canada* 4: 16-27.

Compagnon, Antoine. 1979. *La Seconde main ou le travail de la citation*. Paris: Seuil.

Condé, Mary. 2001. "Japanese Generations in Hiromi Goto's Novel *Chorus of Mush-rooms*". *Etudes Canadiennes/Canadian Studies* 51: 131-43.

Cook, Méira. 1998. "Love and Other Unofficial Stories: Reading Kristjana Gunnars". *Open Letter*, 10, 2: 19-30.

—. 2000. "At the Membane of Language and Silence: Metaphor and Memory in *Fugitive Pieces*". *Canadian Literature* 164 (Spring): 12-33.

Cooke, Nathalie. 1995. "The Politics of Ventriloquism: Margaret Atwood's Fictive Confessions". In Howells, 2000, 140.

Cranny-Francis, Anne. 1990. *Feminist Fiction: Feminist Uses of Generic Fiction*. In Bouson, 8.

Davey, Frank. 1997. "Return to History: Ethnicity and Historiography in Some Re-cent English-Canadian Fiction". *British Journal of Canadian Studies* 12, 1.

Davidoff Leonore and Catherine Hall. 1987. *Family Fortunes: Men and Women of the English Middle Class, 1780-1850*. In Blunt and Rose, 3.

Daurio, Beverley, ed. 1998. *The power to bend spoons: interviews with Canadian novelists*. Toronto: The Mercury Press.

Davidson, Arnold E. 1994. *Coyote Country: Fictions of the Canadian West*. Durham/London: Duke University Press.

Deleuze, Gilles, and Felix Guattari. 1975. *Kafka:Pour une littérature mineure*. Paris: Minuit.

—. 1980. *Mille Plateaux*. Paris: Minuit.

Derrida, Jacques. 1967. *L'Ecriture et la Différence*. Paris: Seuil.

Douglas, Mary. 1969. *Purity and Danger*. In Butler, 1990a, 132.

Dubois, Philippe. 1990. *L'Acte photographique et autre sens*. In LeBlanc, 201.

Dumont, Marilyn. 1994. "It crosses my mind". *West Coast line* ("Colour. An Issue".) 13, 14 (Spring-Fall): 55.

Dvorak, Marta, ed. 1999. *Lire Margaret Atwood: The Handmaid's Tale*. Rennes: Presses Universitaires de Rennes.

Foucault, Michel. 1980. "Questions on Geography". In Soja, 10.

—. 1980. "Right of Death and Power over Life". In Butler, 2.

—. 1994. "Usage des plaisirs et techniques de soi". In *Michel Foucault: Dits et Ecrits 1954-1988*, IV (1980-88), edited by Daniel Defert and François Ewald, 539-61. Paris: Gallimard.

—. 1994. "Subjectivité et verité". In *Michel Foucault: Dits et Ecrits 1954-1988*, IV (1980-88), 213-18.

Gabilliet, Jean-Paul. 1996. "Parler l'espace national: *Civil Elegies* de Dennis Lee". In *L'espace canadien et ses représentations*, edited by Sylvie Guillaume et al., 199-209. Talence: M.S.H.A.

Gabriel, Barbara. 1994. "Performing Theory, Performing Gender: Critical Postscript". *Essays on Canadian Writing* 54 (Winter): 237-60.

Garber, Marjorie. 1992. *Vested Interests: Cross-dressing and Cultural Anxiety*. New York: Routledge.

Gilmore, Leigh. 1998. "Autobiographics". In *Women, Autobiography, Theory: A Reader*, edited by Sidonie Smith and Julia Watson, 183-9. Wisconsin: The University of Wisconsin Press.

Godard, Barbara. 1987. "Structuralism/Post-Structuralism: Language, Reality and Canadian Literature". In *Future Indicative: Literary Theory and Canadian Litera-ture*, edited by John Moss, 25-51. Ottawa: University of Ottawa Press.

Goldman, Marlene. 1993. "Earth-quaking the Kingdom of the Male Virgin: A Deleuzian Analysis of Aritha van Herk's *No Fixed Address* and *Places Far From Ellesmere*". *Canadian Literature* 137 (Summer]: 21-38.

Goto, Hiromi. 1994. *Chorus of Mushrooms*. Edmonton: NeWest Press.

Gould, Karen. 1992. "Féminisme, postmodernité, esthétique de lecture: *Le désert mauve* de Nicole Brossard". In *Le Roman Québecois depuis 1960*, edited by Louise Milot and Jaap Lintvelt, 195-211. Sainte-Foy: Presses de l'Université de Laval.

Guillaume, Sylvie et al, eds. 1996. *L'espace canadien et ses représentations*. Talence: M.S.H.A.

Grace, Sherrill E. 1995. "'Franklin Lives': Atwood's Northern Ghosts". *Various Atwoods: Essays on the Later Poems, Short Fiction and Novels*, edited by Lorraine M. York, 146-66. Concord, Ontario: Anansi.

Gunew, Sneja. 1985. "Migrant Women Writers: Who's on Whose Margins?" In Wong, 124.

—. 1998. "Operatic Karaoke and The Pitfalls of Identity Politics". In *Literary Pluralities*, edited by Christl Verduyn, 254-62. Peterborough: Broadview Press.

Gunnars, Kristjana. 1989. *The Prowler*. Red Deer, Alberta: Red Deer College Press.

Hanson, Claire, ed. 1989. *Re-Reading the Short Story*. London: Macmillan.

Harris, Claire. 1994. "Why do I Write?" In *Grammar of Dissent*, edited by Carol Morrell, 26-33. Fredericton: Goose Lane Editions.

Harris, Wilson. 1991. Interview by Kirsten Holst Petersen and Anna Rutherford. "Some intimations of the Stranger". In *Wilson Harris: The Uncompromising Imagination*, edited by Hene Maes Jelinek, 27-30. Sydney/Mundelstrup: Dangaroo Press.

Harrison, Dick. 1977. *Unnamed Country: The Struggle for a Canadian Prairie Fiction*. Edmonton: The University of Alberta Press.

Hassoun, Jacques. 1994. *Les Contrebandiers de la Mémoire*. Paris: Syros.

Heffernan, Teresa. 1992. "Tracing the Travesty: Constructing the Female Subject in Susan Swan's *The Biggest Modern Woman of the World*". *Canadian Literature* 133: 24-37.

Heim, Otto. 1999. "Reading off the Map, or: What, and Where, Is Experience in the Writing of Aritha van Herk and M. Nourbese Philip?" in *Theory and Literary Creation*, edited by Jean-Pierre Durix, 129-44. Dijon: Editions Universitaires de Dijon.

Holbrook, Susan. 1997. "Mauve Arrows and the Erotics of Translation". *Essays on Canadian Writing* 61: 232-41.

Howells, Coral Ann. 1987. *Private and Fictional Words: Canadian women novelists of the 1970s and 1980s*. London/New York: Menthuen.

—. 1995. "It all depends on where you stand in relation to the forest": Atwood and the Wilderness from *Surfacing* to *Wilderness Tips*. In *Various Atwoods: Essays on the Later Poems, Short Fiction and Novels*, edited by Lorraine M. York, 47-70. Concord, Ontario: Anansi.

—. 1996. *Margaret Atwood*. Basingstoke: Macmillan.

—. 2000. "Transgressing Genre: A Generic Approach to Margaret Atwood's Novels". In *Margaret Atwood: Works and Impact*, edited by Reingard M. Nischik, 139-56. Rochester, New York: Camden House.

Huggan, Graham. 1991. "Decolonizing the Map: Postcolonialism, Post-Structuralism and the Cartographic Connection". In *Past the Last Post: Theorizing Postcolonialism and Post-Modernism,* edited by Ian Adam and Helen Tiffin, 125-38. New York: Harvester Wheatsheaf.

—. 1994. *Territorial Disputes: Maps and Mapping Strategies in Contemporary Canadian and Australian Fiction*. Toronto: University of Toronto Press.

Hutcheon, Linda. 1988. *The Canadian Postmodern: A Study of Contemporary English-Canadian Fiction*. Toronto: Oxford University Press.

Hutcheon, Linda, and Marion Richmond, eds. 1990. *Other Solitudes: Canadian Multicultural Fictions*. Toronto: Oxford University Press.

Hutcheon, Linda. 1991. *Splitting Images: Contemporary Canadian Ironies*. Don Mills, Ontario: Oxford University Press.

—. 1991. "Circling the Downspout of Empire". In Brydon, 193.

Irigaray, Luce. [1977] 1981. "This Sex Which is not One". In *New French Feminisms: An Anthology*, edited by Elaine Marks and Isabelle de Courtivron, 99-110. Brighton: Harvester.

Irvine, Lorna. 2000. "Kitsch, Camp, and Trash in Atwood's Fiction". In *Margaret Atwood: Works and Impact*, edited by Reingard M. Nischik, 202-14. Rochester, NY.

Itwaru, Arnold Harrichand. 1990. *The invention of Canada: Literary Text and the Immigrant Imaginary*. Toronto: TSAR.

Jelinek, Hene Maes, ed. 1991. *Wilson Harris: The Uncompromising Imagination*. Sydney/Mundelstrup: Dangaroo Press.

Kamboureli, Smaro. 2000. *Scandalous Bodies: Diasporic Literature in English Canada*. Don Mills, Ontario: Oxford University Press.

—. 2001. "Denise Chong's The Concubine's Children: Modernity and Postethnicity". Talk given at the Marburg Canadian Literature Day, Marburg, June 13th.

Kaplan, Caren. 1998. "Resisting Autobiography: Out-Law Genres and Transnational Feminist Subjects". In *Women, Autobiography, Theory: A Reader*, edited by Sidonie Smith and Julia Watson, 208-16. Wisconsin: The University of Wisconsin Press.

Kogawa, Joy. [1981] 1983. *Obasan*. Toronto: Penguin.

Krishnaswamy, Revathi. 1999. "Mythologies of Migrancy: Postcolonialism, Postmodernism and the Politics of (Dis)location". In McCallum and Olbey, 165-6.

Kristeva, Julia. 1980. *Pouvoirs de l'horreur*. In Braidotti, 81.

—. 1982. *Desire in Language: A Semiotic Approach to Literature and Art*. Oxford: Basil Blackwell.

Kroestch, Robert. 1983. "Unhiding the Hidden: Recent Canadian Fiction". *Open Letter* 5, 4: 17-21.

—. 1983. " On Being an Alberta Writer". *Open Letter* 5, 4: 69-80.

—. 1983. "The Fear of Women in Prairie Fiction: an Erotics of Space". *Open Letter* 5, 4: 47-56.

Langer, Lawrence L. 1991. *Holocaust Testimonies: The Ruins of Memory*. New Haven/London: Yale University Press.

Lau, Evelyn. [1989] 1996. *Runaway: Diary of a Street Kid*. Toronto: HarperPerrenial.

—. 1995. *Other Women*. London: Minerva.

LeBlanc, Julie. 1993. "Le système pictural de *Volkswagen Blues* de Jacques Poulin: du signifiant de l'image au signifié du texte". In *Image et Récit: Littérature(s) et Arts Visuels du Canada*, edited by Jean-Michel Lacroix et al, 195-208. Paris: Presses de la Sorbonne Nouvelle.

Lee, Sky. [1990] 1991. *Disappearing Moon Cafe*. Vancouver: Douglas & McIntyre.

Lent, John. 1991. "Staring into Snow: Subjectivity and Design in Kristjana Gunnars' *The Prowler*". *RANAM*, XXIV: 103-15.

Libin, Mark. 1999. "Lost in Translation: Hiromi Goto's *Chorus of Mushrooms*". *Canadian Literature* 163 (Winter): 121-40.

Loriggio, Francesco. 1987. "The Question of the Corpus: Ethnicity and Canadian Literature". *Future Indicative: Literary Theory and Canadian Literature*, edited by John Moss, 53-69. Ottawa. University of Ottawa Press.

Mayr, Suzette. 1998. *The Widows*. Edmonton: NeWest Press.

McCallum, Pamela, and Christian Olbey. 1999. "Written in the Scars: History, Genre and Materiality in Dionne Brand's *In Another Place, Not Here*". *Canadian Literature*, 68 (Fall): 159-82.

McGregor, Gaile. 1985. *The Wacousta Syndrome: Explorations in the Canadian Langscape*. In Hutcheon, 1991, 4.

Melville, Pauline. 1992. *Daughters of Africa*. In Welsh, 146.

Merivale, Patricia. 1995. "From 'Bad News' to 'Good Bones': Margaret Atwood's Gendering of Art and Elegy". In *Various Atwoods: Essays on the Later Poems, Short Fiction and Novels*, edited by Lorraine M. York, 253-70. Concord, Ontario: Anansi.

Michaels, Anne. [1996] 1997. *Fugitive Pieces*. London: Bloomsbury.

Miller, Nancy K. 1981. "Emphasis Added: Plots and Plausibilities in Women's Fiction". In Bouson, 6.

Miki, Roy. 1998. *Broken Entries: Race, Subjectivity, Writing*. Toronto: The Mercury Press.

Mohanty, Chandra Talpade. 1987. "Feminist Encounters: Locating the Politics of Experience". In Blunt and Rose, 7.

Morrell, Carol, ed.1994. *Grammar of Dissent*. Fredericton: Goose Lane Editions.

Moss, John, ed. 1987. *Future Indicative: Literary Theory and Canadian Literature*. Ottawa: University of Ottawa Press.

Mott, Asta. 1998. "Aritha van Herk's *Places Far From Ellesmere*: The Wild and Adventurous North?" *Canadian Literature* 157 (Summer): 99-111.

Moore, Henrietta L. 1988. *Space Text Gender: An Anthropological Study of the Marakwet of Kenya*. In Blunt and Rose, 3.

Mukherjee, Arun. 1994. *Oppositional Aesthetics: Readings from a Hyphenated Space*. Toronto: TSAR Publications.

Mycak, Sonia. 1996. *In Search of the Split Subject: Psychanalysis, Phenomenology, and the Novels of Margaret Atwood*. Toronto: ECW Press.

Narain, Denise deCaires. 1999. "The Body of the Woman in the Body of the Text: the Novels of Erna Brodber". In *Caribbean Women Writers: Fiction in English*, edited by Mary Condé and Thorunn Lonsdale, 97-116. Basingstoke/London: Macmillan Press.

Neher, André. 1970. *L'Exil de la parole: Du silence biblique au silence d'Auschwitz*. Paris: Seuil.

Neuman, Shirley. 1996. "Writing the Reader; Writing the Self in Aritha van Herk's *Places Far from Ellesmere*". *Essays on Canadian Writing* 60: 215-34.

Newton, Esther. 1972. *Mother Camp: Female Impersonators in America*. In Butler, 1990, 137.

Nischik, Reingard M., ed. 2000. *Margaret Atwood: Works and Impact*. Rochester, NY: Camden House.

Oiwa, Keibo, ed. 1991. *Stone Voices: Wartime Writings of Japanese Canadian Issei*. Montréal: Véhicule Press.

Oltarzewska, Jagna. 1999. "Strategies for Bearing Witness: Testimony as Construct in Margaret Atwood's *The Handmaid's Tale*. In *Lire Margaret Atwood: The Handmaid's Tale*, edited by Marta Dvorak, 47-55. Rennes: Presses Universitaires de Rennes.

Omhovère Claire. 2002a. "Wandering Tropes or Geography in Anne Michaels's *Fugitive Pieces* (1996)". *Collection de l'AFEC* 6 ("Lecture(s) du paysage canadien"): 103-16.

—. 2002b. "The North in Rudy Wiebe's *A Discovery of Strangers* A Land Beyond Words?" *Commonwealth* 24, 2: 79-91.

—. 2002c. "Sasquatch Quatsch: Cultural Hybridity in Suzette Mayr's *The Widows*". *Marburger Kanada-Studien* ("Writing Canadians: The Literary Construction of Ethnic Identities") 1: 121-33.

Patterson, Janet. 1993. *Moments Postmodernes dans le roman québécois*. Ottawa: Les Presses de l'Université d'Ottawa.

Phelan, Peggy. 1993. *Unmarked: the Politics of Performance*. London: Routledge.

Philip, M. Nourbese. 1989. "The Absence of Writing or How I Almost Became a Spy". In *Grammar of Dissent*, edited by Carol Morrell, 98-104. Fredericton: Goose Lane Editions.

Poster, Mark, ed. 1988. *Jean Baudrillard: Selected Writings*. Cambridge: Polity Press.

Rao, Eleonora. 1993. *Strategies for Identity: The Fiction of Margaret Atwood.* New York: Peter Lang.

Renk, Kathleen J. 1999. *Caribbean Shadows and Victorian Ghosts: Women's Writing and Decolonization*. Charlottesville/London: University Press of Virginia.

Ricou, Laurence. 1973. *Vertical Man/Horizontal World: Man and Landscape in Canadian Prairie Fiction*. Vancouver: University of British Columbia Press.

Ricoeur, Paul. 1975. *La Métaphore vive*. Paris: Seuil.

Robinson, Arthur H., and Barbara Bartz Petchenik. 1976. *The Nature of Maps: towards Understanding Maps and Mapping*. In van Herk, 1992, 57.

Rody, Caroline. 2001. *The Daughter's Return: African-American and Caribbean Women's Fictions of History*. New York: Oxford University Press.

Ross, Sinclair. [1941] 1957. *As For Me and My House*. Toronto: McClelland and Stewart.

Rowe, Percy. 1976. *Niagara Falls and Falls*. In Mayr, 191.

Scott, Gail. 1989. *Spaces Like Stairs*. Toronto: The Women's Press.

Schama, Simon. 1995. *Landscape and Memory*. London: Harper Collins.

Serres, Michel. 1983. *Rome, le livre des fondations*. In Omhovère, 2002c, 131.

Siemerling, Winfried. 1994. *Discoveries of the Other: Alterity in the Work of Leonard Cohen, Hubert Aquin, Michael Ondaatje and Nicole Brossard.* Toronto: University of Toronto Press.

Simon, Sherry. 1992. "The Language of cultural difference: Figures of alterity in Canadian translation". In *Rethinking Translation: Discourse, Subjectivity, Ideology*, edited by Lawrence Venuti, 159-76. London /New York: Routledge.

Slemon, Stephen and Helen Tiffin, eds. 1989. *After Europe: Critical Theory and Post-Colonial Writing*. Sydney/Mundelstrup: Dangaroo Press.

Smart, Patricia. 1988. *Ecrire dans la maison du père: L'émergence du féminin dans la tradition littéraire du Québec*. Montréal: Editions Québec/Amérique, 1988.

Smith, Sidonie, and Julia Watson, eds. 1998. *Women, Autobiography, Theory: A Reader*. Wisconsin: The University of Wisconsin Press.

Soja, Edward. 1989. *Postmodern Geographies: The Reassertion of Space in Critical Social Theory*. London/ New York: Verso.

Sontag, Susan. 1961. *Against Interpretation*. New York: Dell.

Stewart, Susan. 1984. *On Longing: Narratives of the Miniature, the Gigantic, the Souvenir, the Collection.* Baltimore/London: The John Hopkins University Press.

Suleri, Sara. 1987. "The Geography of *A Passage to India*". In *E. M. Forster's A Passage to India: Modern Critical Interpretations*, edited by Harold Bloom, 107-13. London: Chelsea House Publishers.

Swan, Susan. [1993] 1994. *The Wives of Bath*. London: Granta.

Taylor, C. 1985. *Philosophy and the Human Sciences*. In Bhabha, 1994, 177.

Tibi, Pierre. 1988. "La Nouvelle: Essai de compréhension d'un genre". *Cahiers de l'Université de Perpignan*: 7-62.

Todorov, Tzvetan. 1976. "The Origin of Genres". *New Literary History*, 8, 1: 159-70.

Tostevin, Lola Lemire. 1989. "Contamination: A Relation of Difference". In Brydon, 1991, 191-203.

van Herk, Aritha. [1986] 1989. *No Fixed Address: An Amorous Journey*. London: Virago.

—. 1990. *Places Far From Ellesmere*. Red Deer, Alberta: Red Deer College Press.

—. 1991. *In Visible Ink (crypto-frictions)*. Edmonton: NeWest Press.

—. 1992. *A Frozen Tongue*. Sydney/Mundelstrup: Dangaroo Press.

—. 1998. Interview by Karin Beeler. "Shifting Form". *Canadian Literature* 157 (Summer): 80-96.

Wagner-Martin, Linda. 1995. "'Giving Way to Bedrock': Atwood's Later Poems". In *Various Atwoods: Essays on the Later Poems, Short Fiction and Novels*, edited by Lorraine M. York, 71-88. Concord, Ontario: Anansi.

Venuti, Lawrence, ed. 1992. *Rethinking Translation: Discourse, Subjectivity, Ideology*, London /New York: Routledge.

Verduyn, Christl, ed. 1998. *Literary Pluralities*. Peterborough: Broadview Press.

Verwaayen, Kimberly. 1997. "Region/Body: In? Of? And? Or? (Alter/Native) Separatism in thePolitics of Nicole Brossard". *Essays on Canadian Writing* 61: 1-16.

Welsh, Sarah Lawson, ed. 1999. "Pauline Melville's Shape-Shifting Fictions". In *Caribbean Women Writers: Fiction in English*, edited by Mary Condé and Thorunn Lonsdale, 144-71. Basingstoke: Macmillan.

Wiens, Jason. 2000. "'Language Seemed to Split in Two': National Ambivalence(s) and Dionne Brand's 'No Language is Neutral'". *Canadian Literature* 70 (Spring): 81-102.

Williamson, Janice. 1993. *Sounding Differences: Conversations with Seventeen Canadian Women Writers*. Toronto: University of Toronto Press.

Wong, Jan. 1997. "Evelyn Lau gets perfect grades in school of hard knocks". *The Globe and Mail* April 3rd: C1.

Wong, Rita. 1995. "Jumping on hyphens – a bricolage receiving 'genealogy/gap, ' 'goods, ' 'east asian canadian, ' 'translation' & 'laughter'". In *The Other Woman: Women of Colour in Contemporary Canadian Literature*, edited by Makeda Silvera, 117-54. Toronto: Sister Vision Press.

—. 2001. "Market Forces and Powerful Desires: Reading Evelyn Lau's Cultural Labour". *Canadian Literature* 73 (Spring): 122-40.

York, Lorraine M, ed. 1995. "'Over All I Place a Glass Bell': The Meta-Iconography of Margaret Atwood". In *Various Atwoods: Essays on the Later Poems, Short Fiction and Novels*, 229-52. Concord, Ontario: Anansi.

Žižek, Slavoj. 1997. *The Plague of Fantasies*. In Beauregard, 58.

Index

A Discovery of Strangers, 35, 36, 153
appropriation, 21, 43, 57, 99, 102, 106, 114, 118
Arctic, 40, 99, 100, 108, 109, 114, 120, 124
As For Me and My House, 21, 153
Ashcroft, 29, 60, 147
Atwood, 11, 15, 16, 20, 26, 39, 47, 121, 122, 123, 124, 125, 126, 127, 128, 129, 130, 132, 133, 141, 144, 147, 148, 149, 150, 151, 152, 153, 154
Auschwitz, 40, 43
authentic, 11, 12, 20, 28, 91, 110, 112, 114, 120
Bakhtin, 30, 73, 147
Barthes, 30, 32, 147
Baudrillard, 38, 147, 153
Beauregard, 33
Beautell, 68, 112, 147
Beloved, 64, 148
Berton, 68, 75
Bhabha, 47, 52, 57, 87, 135, 147
Bhakhtin, 15, 73, 136
Black, 51, 52, 53, 54, 56, 58, 62, 63, 112, 133
Blanchot, 41, 45, 148
Blossom, Priestess of Oya, Goddess of winds, storms and waterfalls, 60
bodily, 33, 71, 89, 94, 130, 140, 144
body, 25, 27, 32, 53, 54, 55, 59, 60, 64, 70, 71, 72, 73, 74, 85, 86, 88, 89, 91, 95, 96, 107, 116, 135, 136, 139, 140, 141, 143
Bourdieu, 131, 148
Bouson, 122, 124, 132, 148, 149, 152
Braidotti, 13, 31, 72, 73, 118, 119, 120, 144, 148, 151

Brand, 15, 16, 32, 39, 48, 51, 52, 53, 54, 55, 56, 57, 58, 59, 60, 61, 62, 63, 64, 143, 144, 148, 152, 154
Brossard, 16, 42, 77, 89, 90, 91, 92, 93, 94, 96, 97, 143, 145, 148, 150, 153, 154
Brydon, 109, 110, 118, 133, 137, 140, 148
Camus, 56
Caribbean, 15, 16, 32, 48, 51, 52, 53, 54, 55, 57, 58, 59, 62, 63, 143, 152, 153, 154
carnivalesque
  carnival, 70, 72, 73, 74, 136
Cartesian, 72, 73
cartography, 99, 103, 104
Cat's Eye, 141
Chorus of Mushrooms, 19, 21, 25, 28, 29, 31, 32, 33, 34, 35, 100, 149, 150, 151
Cixous, 60, 89
Coleman, 113, 148
Compagnon, 29, 148
Condé, 24, 149, 152, 154
contamination, 33, 69, 118, 136
Cook, 110, 117, 149
Creole, 59, 61
cross-cultural, 15, 22, 27, 29, 34, 46, 47, 48, 49, 51, 52, 60, 110, 120, 137, 140, 145
Davey, 19, 149
Davidson, 20, 149
Death by Landscape, 126
deCaires Narain, 59
Deleuze, 28, 90, 149
deterritorialised, 90
difference, 11, 15, 16, 24, 28, 29, 30, 43, 60, 61, 65, 70, 71, 73, 76, 77, 79, 80, 84, 87, 89, 90, 92, 95, 97, 101, 103, 105, 108, 110, 115, 119,

122, 133, 135, 138, 141, 144, 145,
    153
Disappearing Moon Cafe, 88
disappropriation, 103
dislocation, 66, 67, 120
Douglas, 140
Dumont, 54, 149
embodied, 23, 31, 40, 60, 118, 136
enlightenment, 11, 73, 79
ethnic
    ethnicity, 11, 12, 15, 24, 29, 37,
        42, 43, 48, 51, 65, 69, 70, 71,
        73, 74, 78, 79, 84, 95, 121, 144
Eurocentric, 19, 20, 21, 22
f(r)iction, 102
female body, 11, 15, 60, 72, 91, 130,
    133, 141
feminine-centred, 24
feminist, 11, 12, 59, 78, 79, 89, 90,
    91, 121, 132, 133, 144
fiction-theory, 89, 90
Findley, 35, 141
First Nations, 104, 105, 111, 134
Foucault, 22, 80, 135
Franklin, 35, 124, 125, 126, 150
frontier, 20, 45
Fugitive Pieces, 34, 35, 36, 37, 38,
    39, 40, 41, 42, 43, 44, 45, 46, 47,
    49, 111, 149, 152, 153
Gabriel, 14, 140, 149
Garber, 138, 139, 143, 149
garrison, 21, 22, 23, 25
gender, 13, 14, 15, 16, 26, 52, 70, 71,
    73, 89, 122, 123, 130, 133, 135,
    136, 137, 138, 139, 140, 141, 143
genre, 16, 44, 45, 69, 72, 75, 81, 93,
    100, 122, 129, 130, 133, 134, 154
geografictione, 16, 89, 106, 108, 109
geology
    geological, 40, 41, 43, 70
Gilmore, 81, 82, 114, 149
Godard, 14, 149
Goldman, 107, 149
Good Bones, 121, 123, 128, 147, 152
Goto, 15, 16, 19, 20, 21, 22, 23, 24,
    25, 26, 27, 29, 30, 31, 32, 34, 35,
    39, 55, 71, 100, 124, 143, 149,
    150, 151
Gould, 92, 150
Grace, 124, 150
Guattari, 28, 90, 149

Gunnars, 16, 99, 109, 110, 111, 112,
    113, 114, 115, 116, 117, 119, 143,
    149, 150, 151
Hanson, 124, 150
Harris C., 51, 53, 150
Harris W., 60, 150
Hassoun, 41, 42
Heart of Darkness, 57
Heffernan, 135, 136, 150
history, 11, 15, 19, 20, 21, 24, 25, 26,
    29, 30, 32, 34, 37, 39, 41, 42, 43,
    45, 46, 48, 51, 52, 53, 55, 56, 60,
    63, 64, 66, 68, 75, 84, 93, 96, 105,
    108, 109, 110, 111, 113, 122, 124,
    125, 140
Holbrook, 91, 93, 94, 150
Holocaust, 35, 36, 37, 39, 40, 43, 44,
    45, 46, 48, 147, 148, 151
hologram, 89, 92
Howells, 67, 70, 74, 123, 127, 149,
    150
Huggan, 48, 100, 101, 103, 150
humanism, 37, 40
Hutcheon, 68, 121, 144, 151
hybrid, 15, 20, 28, 34, 68, 69, 70, 76,
    80, 109, 120, 122
hybridity, 16, 29, 51, 52, 55, 66, 71,
    78, 95, 120, 137, 143
identity
    feminine
        national, 11, 12, 13, 15, 19, 20,
            21, 26, 27, 29, 30, 31, 33,
            34, 43, 47, 51, 54, 61, 65,
            66, 67, 69, 74, 76, 77, 78,
            79, 80, 81, 86, 88, 92, 93,
            97, 99, 101, 103, 104, 105,
            106, 109, 110, 112, 113,
            114, 115, 116, 118, 119,
            120, 133, 135, 136, 140,
            144
    feminine, 28, 30, 56, 65, 67, 120,
        125, 139 Voir Voir
imaginary, 11, 12, 13, 14, 15, 17, 21,
    23, 34, 35, 49, 52, 53, 54, 55, 56,
    59, 60, 61, 65, 69, 92, 97, 100,
    102, 106, 108, 119, 120, 121, 124,
    127, 136, 140, 144, 145
imperialism
    imperialistic, 12
    imperialist, 21, 61, 134, 140

In Another Place, Not Here, 51, 62, 148, 152
In the Skin of a Lion, 35
inscribe, 23, 29
Irigaray, 89, 95, 128
irony, 15, 20, 121, 128, 133, 144
Itwaru, 11, 83, 84, 122, 151
Jane Eyre, 58, 134
Kafka, 90, 149
Kamboureli, 11, 79, 84, 95, 151
Kogawa, 19 Voir
Kristeva, 72, 73
Kroetsch, 11, 22, 28
Lady Oracle, 133, 141
Langer, 40, 41, 44, 45, 148, 151
Lau, 15, 16, 77, 78, 79, 80, 81, 82, 83, 84, 85, 87, 88, 100, 114, 144, 151, 154
Law-of-the-Father, 84, 87, 96, 97
LeBlanc, 30, 149, 151
Lent, 115, 116, 117, 151
Let us Praise Stupid Women, 128
Libin, 33, 34, 151
Loach, 82
location, 15, 34, 44, 53, 101, 102, 110, 114, 143
Marlatt, 93, 94
Mauve Desert, 89, 90, 91, 92, 93, 94, 95, 96, 97, 148
Mayr, 33, 51, 65, 66, 67, 68, 69, 71, 72, 73, 74, 75, 144, 147, 152, 153
McCallum and Olbey, 62, 63, 64, 151
McGregor, 121
Michaels, 16, 34, 47, 48, 49, 111, 143, 152, 153
middle passage, 16, 52, 54, 61
migrancy
    migrant, 16, 27, 29, 47, 51, 53, 54, 55, 64, 67, 120
Miki, 11, 26, 27, 28, 152
Moodie, 69
Moore, 137, 152
Mukherjee, 53, 57, 152
Multicultural Act, 95
multiculturalism, 11, 30, 69
Munro, 141
Mycak, 122, 152
myth, 20, 21, 23, 25, 27, 43, 52, 55, 69, 74, 124, 126, 129
Mythologies, 30
Nazi, 38, 41, 44

Neuman, 106, 107, 152
New World, 16, 48, 61, 62, 83, 125
Niagara, 65, 66, 69, 70, 74, 75
No Fixed Address, 21, 31, 100, 149
No Rinsed Blue Sky, No Red Flower Fences, 53
nomadic, 31
North, 23, 57, 63, 66, 74, 77, 99, 100, 103, 106, 107, 108, 109, 111, 118, 122, 152, 153
Not Wanted on the Voyage, 141
Obasan, 26, 151
Oiwa, 19, 25, 152
Omhovère, 65, 72, 153
Ondaatje, 35, 153
orality, 22, 55, 59, 60, 61
origin, 20, 28, 93, 94, 95, 135, 139
original, 92, 93, 94, 139
origins, 20, 21, 23, 28, 30, 43, 49, 52, 65, 66, 70, 87, 88, 92, 93, 94, 96, 97, 99, 102, 105, 108, 122, 125
Other, 48, 56, 57, 58, 70, 77, 78, 79, 81, 84, 86, 87, 88, 94, 95, 100, 107, 108, 112, 128, 134, 143, 148, 149, 151, 153, 154
    Othering, 14, 15, 20, 24, 26, 28, 44, 48, 54, 59, 73
Other Women, 84, 86, 87, 151
passage, 48, 87, 92, 93, 94, 124
Passage to India, 57, 154
Phelan, 85, 86, 153
Philip, 51, 54, 150, 153
Photograph, 59, 60
pioneer, 22
Places Far From Ellesmere, 99, 100, 102, 149, 152, 154
postcolonial, 11, 12, 14, 29, 31, 52, 60, 61, 64, 78, 79, 87, 101, 109, 112, 121, 144, 145, 147
prairie, 20, 21, 22, 23, 24, 28, 31, 100, 103, 105, 107, 143
race, 13, 48, 52, 54, 57, 110, 123
realism, 23, 24, 61, 88, 96, 106, 144
reinvention, 31, 51, 67, 75, 120
Renk, 55, 56, 57, 60, 153
representation, 11, 12, 13, 14, 15, 17, 22, 23, 30, 34, 41, 44, 45, 53, 54, 57, 59, 63, 67, 70, 73, 74, 77, 79, 81, 82, 83, 85, 86, 87, 89, 92, 93, 94, 95, 100, 104, 105, 106, 108,

109, 112, 113, 114, 115, 117, 118, 122, 123, 127
Ricoeur, 46, 153
Ricou, 21, 22, 153
Ross, 21, 22, 153
Runaway, 77, 80, 82, 86, 151
Sans Souci, 51, 53, 62, 148
Scott, 44, 96
self, 11, 13, 14, 15, 20, 23, 25, 26, 32, 33, 38, 42, 47, 48, 49, 51, 53, 56, 57, 65, 67, 70, 77, 78, 80, 81, 82, 83, 84, 85, 86, 87, 92, 93, 95, 99, 100, 101, 102, 103, 106, 107, 108, 111, 112, 113, 114, 116, 118, 120, 123, 124, 126, 130, 143, 145, 152
Serres, 72, 153
Siemerling, 89, 94, 153
Sky Lee, 88
slavery, 51, 52, 56, 58, 59, 62, 64
Smart, 59, 93, 97, 153
Sontag, 132, 153
St Mary's Estate, 58
subject, 13, 14, 16, 19, 20, 25, 26, 27, 28, 31, 34, 35, 39, 40, 41, 45, 46, 49, 52, 53, 55, 61, 77, 80, 81, 82, 83, 84, 85, 86, 87, 88, 89, 96, 97, 104, 107, 108, 112, 114, 115, 118, 119, 127, 132, 139, 141, 144, 145, 150, 152
subjective, 26, 29, 32, 34, 44, 45, 46, 47, 49, 51, 53, 54, 56, 60, 63, 64, 67, 68, 77, 84, 85, 86, 87, 90, 94, 97, 100, 101, 102, 106, 108, 110, 113, 117, 118, 131, 136, 139, 143, 144, 145
subjectivity, 13, 14, 25, 26, 27, 28, 29, 31, 46, 55, 65, 71, 73, 80, 88, 89, 90, 92, 115, 120, 122, 123, 128, 131, 135, 144, 145
Surfacing, 11, 122, 123, 147
Survival, 26, 122, 147
Swan, 15, 16, 121, 133, 134, 135, 136, 137, 138, 139, 140, 141, 143, 150, 154
symbolic, 13, 14, 16, 44, 52, 55, 59, 65, 73, 76, 77, 79, 84, 85, 86, 87, 89, 90, 91, 95, 96, 97, 99, 106,

109, 110, 117, 119, 128, 136, 137, 139, 144
Taylor, 66, 67, 69, 154
teleological, 24, 69, 108
The Aerial Letter, 89, 148
The Age of Lead, 124, 126, 147
The Female Body, 128, 130
The Handmaid's Tale, 39, 130, 147, 149, 152
The Lisbon Plate, 55
The Lover, 115
The Prowler, 99, 109, 110, 112, 113, 114, 115, 116, 117, 118, 119, 120, 122, 148, 150, 151
The Widows, 16, 33, 51, 65, 69, 70, 73, 76, 152, 153
The Wives of Bath, 133, 134, 135, 136, 137, 139, 140, 141, 154
Tibi, 124, 154
Todorov, 126, 154
Tolstoy, 107, 108
Tostevin, 118, 154
Trail, 69
translation, 16, 25, 27, 31, 47, 65, 77, 92, 93, 94, 97, 153, 154
True Trash, 130
Unpopular Gals, 128
van Herk, 16, 21, 23, 31, 89, 99, 100, 101, 104, 105, 106, 107, 108, 109, 113, 124, 143, 145, 149, 150, 152, 154
Verwaayen, 90, 96, 154
White, 16, 52, 54, 55, 57, 62, 100
Wide Sargasso Sea, 58
Wiebe, 35, 153
Wiens, 59, 61, 154
wilderness, 20, 67, 69, 74, 126
Wilderness Tips, 121, 123, 147, 150
Woman, 89, 107, 128, 129, 135, 136, 150, 152, 154
women's writing, 13, 14, 17, 59, 133
Wong, 78, 150, 154
York, 123, 129, 147, 148, 149, 150, 153, 154
Žižek, 79, 154